Scenes and Monologues for Young Actors

Compiled and Edited

by

KENT R. BROWN

Dramatic Publishing
Woodstock, Illinois • England • Australia • New Zealand

Published by The Dramatic Publishing Company
P.O. Box 129, Woodstock, IL 60098

©MM by
KENT R. BROWN

Printed in the United States of America
All Rights Reserved
(SCENES AND MONOLOGUES FOR YOUNG ACTORS)

Cover design by Susan Carle

ISBN 0-87129-958-5

ACKNOWLEDGMENTS

Dramatic Publishing wishes to acknowledge the contributions Roger Bedard and Jeanne Averill have made to this collection. Special thanks is extended to Cynthia L. Brown of Mesa High School in Mesa, Arizona, for her guidance and expertise.

CONTENTS

DUETS

SCENES WITH MULTIPLE CHARACTERS

MONOLOGUES FOR MEN

MONOLOGUES FOR WOMEN

INTRODUCTION

Welcome to **Scenes and Monologues for Young Actors**, a contemporary anthology featuring over 125 challenging roles written for young actors. The material is diverse in the range of its subject matter and tone. **Scenes and Monologues for Young Actors** is geared to the classroom environment, allowing drama instructors to assign work of varying complexity to advanced as well as beginning students. The selections are intended to sharpen an actor's skills in the area of concentration, characterization and performance consistency. The anthology can also be used as a resource for auditions and forensic competitions.

An attractive feature is the inclusion of scenes for more than two actors. **Welcome to McDonald's** and **Meatballs**, for example, integrate multiple roles for men and women. Other selections, including **Hoagy Fredmeister, Told Her** and **Teamplay**, all require four or more actors and will aid greatly in developing strong ensemble skills. Additional pieces, such as **The Bag of Chips, Cue to Cue** and **The Go-Go Girl**, will serve well as exercises in point of view, cue pickup and timing. Other scenes and monologues, such as **Between the Lines, Benediction, Lessons for Life, X-Man** and **The Right Box** among others, will invite more thoughtful and sensitive analyses of human motivation.

Good theatre is created only through dedication and a willingness to learn. An actor's task is to interpret behavior, analyze dramatic conflict and convince an audience that real stakes are involved in the outcome of the action. Only through skillful and imaginative performances will an audience perceive the theatre as not only entertaining, but necessary to their daily lives.

Interspersed throughout the book, you will find a series of suggestions, observations and reminders intended to aid in developing effective acting and performance skills.

I hope they will be helpful. Good luck and good acting!

Kent R. Brown
May 1999

TIPS FOR THE ACTOR

YOU AND THE PLAY

• In its most elemental state, a challenging play will focus primarily on one central character who makes a conscious decision to journey—psychologically and emotionally—from point "A" to point "B" in order to achieve an objective. The journey will then be blocked by an obstacle—usually another character or your central character's psychological imperfections—thus forcing your central character to make further choices and initiate actions to overcome the obstacle. The vast majority of plays are constructed around this dramatic equation.

• In addition, it will not be easy for characters to achieve their objectives. They will fight, claw, lie, plead, cheat, love, withhold, release, bargain, sacrifice themselves or barter with the enemy—anything to reach point "B." After all, it's not easy for those of us in the audience to get through our lives; so why should dramatic characters have it any better. In short, then: No conflict—no interest; no interest—no applause! Remember, audiences come to witness two or more real people locked in a struggle of conflicting needs and desires.

• But good scene work is far more than merely delivering well-memorized lines. It must be infused with a sense of reality, of immediacy. It must reverberate with behavior the audience believes is true to life.

• Analyze the play, scene or monologue with the assumption that everything is there for an express purpose—the words, the silences, the set and costume descriptions and the stage business. Playwriting is a precise craft, and in well-written material all words and actions fit together to the overall benefit of the text and the performer.

• Pay close attention to the language your character uses to help discover your character's attitude toward others and toward life in general. Is your character irascible, charming, deceitful, naïve, compassionate, sullen, exuberant, insensitive, blunt or evasive? How does your character respond to being teased, ignored, thwarted, accepted, confused, loved or challenged?

• Just as in life, don't always assume the characters in the play are telling the full truth at any moment. They may be diverting attention, withholding key pieces of information or outright lying. Your task is to discover the underlying truth of the dramatic situation and determine why the characters, perhaps, are not telling the complete truth.

• Characters, like real people, are very complex. Their true nature is revealed through what they say, by what others say about them and by what the characters actually do. In the theatre, what a character does is usually of greatest importance. Remember, acting is about actions, not about speeches. The key is discovering what actions your character needs to take to be effective in the scene.

CHARACTER ANALYSIS CHECKLIST

Just saying lines with energy and volume will not make you a respected actor. Good acting requires diligent preparation and a respect for the script, for your fellow actors and for all who contribute to the production. By answering the following questions precisely, you will be taking the correct steps to portraying your character with intelligence and imagination.

What Does Your Character Want to Achieve?

- Acting is psychology in action. It is about behaving in ways to accomplish objectives, just as you are doing in your personal life. If you want to belong to a special group, chances are you will act as the group does and share in the group's activities. If you want to belong to an athletic team, you will take time from your busy schedule to train properly so you can maximize your eligibility to make the squad. You learn to make specific choices to achieve your goals. Characters must behave like real people, and actors must be ready to analyze their characters' objectives.

- Theatre is quite different from life. It is intensified. It only has a handful of minutes to throw characters into conflict and see who will emerge victorious. The more specific your "want" is, the more purposeful your acting will be. And the more you need to achieve your goal *now*, the more the scene or monologue will be charged with a sense of urgency.

- Avoid "wanting" states of "being" such as "I want to be happy." States of being are too often passive, lacking in tension. Tension creates interest on the stage and in real life as well. Listen to how we speak about our lives. "What are you *doing* this Friday night?" "What are you going to *do* about being grounded?" "I don't know what I'll *do* if Bobby doesn't call/if I don't make the team/if I don't get paid this Saturday." Notice how time-intense these statements are. We seldom say "I don't know what I'll do if I've never traveled to China by the time I'm fifty years of age." Of course not. Your concerns about yourself at age fifty can be postponed until you're much older. But today is now, and that is how we all tend to live our lives.

• Phrase your character's "want" in a single sentence, and take personal ownership of that desire. Instead of saying "My character wants a glass of water," say instead "I want a glass of water." Or, instead of saying "My character wants to be loved," say instead "I want my mother/father/companion to respect my opinions." We all want to be loved, but working specifically toward having our opinions valued is far more tangible. By taking ownership of your character's desires and needs, you will feel energized and personally invested in the outcome of the action.

• If you don't know what your character "wants," then your acting will be vague, general and lacking in definition and clarity. Ambivalence is not dramatic or theatrically effective. Theatre is about passion, not about indetermination.

Why Does Your Character Want to Achieve the Objective?

• It is not enough to know what your character wants to achieve. You have to know why your character wants to achieve his or her goal. The motivations behind our desires are often far more interesting than the goal we are striving toward. So, how about you? Why do you shy away from certain people at school and gravitate toward other groups? Why do you want the best grade you can get in algebra or biology or Spanish? Just to add to your accomplishments? Or are you trying to impress your parents, or your uncle, or your boss at your part-time job who doesn't think you'll ever amount to anything?

• As people, we tend to seek confirmation and acceptance, we desire to be respected rather than disrespected, loved rather than unloved, and so on. But sometimes we have to endure discomfort in order to achieve a goal that is worth that discomfort. We have to make choices about how we are going to be perceived by others as well as by ourselves. Your task is to look beneath the surface of daily human behavior and uncover the essential motivation behind why we behave as we do. "I want more allowance money" is not as interesting to play as "I want Mom to give me more responsibility," or "I want Mom to recognize what I do for her." The allowance money is only a symbol of something deeper and richer. As stated previously, acting is psychology in action. And psychology is the study of behavior and motivation.

• Avoid being glib and slick. Chances are the first choice you make about why your character behaves in a certain way will be only surface thin. The first choice may be the easiest but also the most general choice you can make. Life may be rambling and fuzzy at times but the theatre must never be out of focus. Theatre demands precision and clarity. Actors serve as the audience's guides through the life of the play.

• In real life, if you say, "I don't know why I said that (or did that)," you often can avoid taking responsibility for those thoughts or actions. If, however, you answer "I don't know" when the director asks you why your character says or does something in the play, then you're relinquishing your special insights as an artist. Take responsibility for your talent. Engage your mind and your heart.

What Obstacles Keep Your Character from Achieving the Objective?

• If your character easily achieves his or her objective, the audience will feel cheated. Audiences come to witness your character running an obstacle course, and the audience wants to witness a challenging race to the finish line. If the obstacles are inconsequential, then the race has no intrinsic tension.

• Obstacles usually fall into one of three categories. The first category includes external or physical obstacles: a blizzard, crop failure or failing health. Your character must deal with the difficulties these physical obstacles create. The second category includes a blocking character, the antagonist, who is intent on stopping your character from successfully accomplishing his or her objective: a domineering parent or spouse, a vengeful employer at work, a jealous sibling or a teacher or fellow student at school. The third category, highly prevalent in contemporary playwriting, includes your character's own failings and limitations: self-doubt, fear of rejection or physical pain, uncertainty, vanity, arrogance, stubbornness or lack of compassion.

• This last category provides the most fertile opportunities to apply your analytical skills. And where do you look to discover truthful human emotions and reactions? At yourself, of course, and those you know well. Differences among people are far fewer than we think. We all need food and shelter, we all desire comfort and a sense of belonging. And we have all been left out of a group, desired something we've never received or have behaved unfairly toward another person. To reach a fuller understanding of the complex nature of human behavior, actors must tap into their own hearts and souls. Remember, truthful acting will reflect your regard for the playwright and the audience far more than cheap gimmicks and easy laughs.

• Respect the antagonist in the play, scene or monologue you perform. Always look for ways in which the playwright has tried to humanize the "bad guy." If you trivialize your opponent, you trivialize your character's quest. You must give the antagonist a full life with legitimate needs and objectives.

What Actions Does Your Character Take to Overcome the Obstacles?

• Notice this section addresses the "actions taken" by your character to overcome obstacles; it says nothing about "words spoken." There is a tendency to rely too heavily on the "lines" in a play or a scene. In real life, it is what we *do* that says volumes about who we are. You are taking steps (actions) to improve your acting by enrolling in an acting course, attending productions, even reading this book. You are not just saying "I wish I could be an actor." You are saying "I am reading a book on acting" and thereby "taking action." Your character should be doing the same thing—taking action to achieve an objective. Remember, the word "acting" comes from the word "action" not the word "talk."

• Consider the lines your character speaks as the tips of the motivational iceberg. They represent ideas and strategies your character employs to move the obstacles aside and achieve the objective. Words will sound ungrounded and feel disconnected from the character if delivered without an understanding of the intention behind them.

• Consider what character "business" you could employ that would convey nonverbally how your character feels and thinks at any given moment. Don't wait for the playwright to provide all your strategies. Be imaginative, inventive. But also be consistent with your character's environment and state of mind. If your scene takes place in a bedroom, your character might be cleaning vigorously in order to avoid facing a particular problem, or your character might be bouncing a tennis ball or practicing hockey shots with a broom and an old sock. If a monologue takes place in a storeroom, perhaps your character could be tearing down cardboard boxes, stacking chairs. In other words, look for actions and behavior that will reinforce the emotions your character is experiencing.

• Be selective in the number and variety of strategies your character employs. Don't take one strategy and run it into the ground, such as yelling all your lines if you are angry or whining if you are displeased. People are far more diverse in real life. We cajole, tease, bully, seduce, sweet-talk, insinuate, plead, demand and negotiate our way through life every day. Also, people seldom yell, or if they do they seldom keep at it. Yelling is tiring and takes energy away from the hard job of maintaining good concentration and listening skills.

What Stakes Are Involved and What Is Your Character Willing to Give Up to Achieve the Objective?

• We all "put up with" something to get something else in life. We sometimes feel we have to "put up with school" in order to get the graduation diploma that will be our key to the next phase of our lives. These trade-offs are sometimes uncomfortable or downright frustrating: taking out the trash, giving some of our hard-earned money to parents to help with living expenses, watching our younger sister when we want to be with our friends, and so on. Life is full of trade-offs. Your character, willingly or not, faces similar choices. And the audience wants to see high stakes involved in your character's life.

• Theatre, whether serious or comic in nature, is about conditions of discomfort and desperation and about people who are no longer willing to remain in those situations. Seldom is good theatre about a family with no problems, lots of money, happy and well-adjusted children, aunts and uncles. Life, far from being stable or predictable, is often chaotic, full of emotional potholes. And, for the most part, we seem to like the energy and adventure that life's inconsistencies bring to us. Our work on the stage must mirror the struggle to live successfully in our daily lives.

• Discover what your character values. When those values come under attack, chances are your character will begin to take action. In contemporary drama, most of the stakes center on human relationships: a valued trust that is broken between two friends, siblings or a married couple. Perhaps a friend has lied about you. Why? How did you hurt that friend, or what does your friend hope to achieve by telling a lie about you? Does your character choose to put his or her emotional well-being at risk in order to help another character? Does your character elect to sacrifice one kind of relationship in favor of another? What are the consequences of making one choice over another? Remember, the inner quality of most people is revealed by the choices they make. And there are consequences every step of the way.

 • If you don't know how high the stakes are and what your character is willing to give up in order to achieve the objective, then the audience will lose interest. Audiences will know when you are holding back. If they believe you don't care about the outcome of the struggle, then why should they? Remember, theatre is a lot like life: no pain, no gain.

PREPARING THE SCENE

The following suggestions are offered as an aid to breathing life-like reality into your scene work.

• When you are rehearsing your scene, it is useful to vary your energy intensity as you vary your strategies. Don't attack all the lines with the same attitude. Maybe you can ease into a controversial discussion, or approach the dramatic problem as a "no problem" problem. Your purpose is to get the other character to do something you want done. Don't beat that character to death by being too aggressive. You might actually make that character pull away from you in a desire to avoid your anger.

• Don't play the end of the scene before you get there. As actors, you will know the outcome of the scene your characters are in. But your characters do not know the outcome and must be attentive to each sound and silence during the scene so they can gather all the information and strength they need to play truthfully their characters' needs and desires.

• Integrate pieces of stage business into your rehearsal so you will feel natural and grounded in the scene when it comes time to perform it. Remember, too, that props in a play are just that—props. They may be a real kitchen towel or a garden rake or a deck of cards, but they have to be more than that on the stage. They have to further illuminate the inner feelings of the character.

Look for the Power Shifts in the Scene

• Good drama is like an exciting athletic competition. No one really wants to watch a lopsided game. We want the contest to be close with the leads changing frequently before the final outcome is known. Audiences come to watch a struggle of wills, a contest of two energies. They don't come to watch a blowout.

• Make your acting more life-like by discovering those moments in the scene when power, influence and/or dominance shifts from one character to the other. See who has the "upper hand" in an argument or who has the "high ground." Determine how your character feels and thinks about the power shifts. What does your character do to gain an advantage so his or her objective will be more successfully achieved?

Look for the Love in the Scene

• A scene about anger or hate is most likely a scene about lost love of one kind or another. Most of the pain in life comes in the departures we've experienced: the loss of loved ones and friends, the loss of feeling close and needed by someone. We respond by feeling defeated, perplexed, angry, frustrated, frightened and even amazed.

• As people, we seldom yell when we are deeply angry. We might talk slowly, in a disarmingly quiet voice, or speak condescendingly or even laugh defensively. We often search for the right word to describe how we feel and then become more frustrated at our inability to find the precise expression. Consequently, a "fight" scene may really be a "love" scene "gone bad." What we are really doing is trying to understand what went wrong so we can fix it, reestablish a positive connection with someone.

A Word or Two About Comedy

• Actors often say, when cast in a comedy, "Oh, good, this will be easy and I'll have a lot of fun." Well, you should certainly have fun, but comedy is far from easy. Don't make the mistake of thinking that comedy is light, fluffy and trivial. Good comic writing examines very serious issues. **The Odd Couple** by Neil Simon, for example, is a serious play about how selfish behaviors can destroy a solid and wonderful friendship.

• Good comic lines derive from the ironic viewpoint the characters have of themselves, their predicament and the prospects of surviving the situation.

• Most of us are unaware of our annoying, endearing or funny habits, phrases and attitudes. As a three-dimensional character in a "real" make-believe situation, be sure you don't telegraph the "funny" moments to the audience.

• When you play a character in a comedy, be sure you go through the same Character Checklist you do when cast in a serious drama. Be sure you know what your character wants and what the stakes are. Even though comedy puts the spotlight on character foibles, you should not think you, as the actor/character, are funny. The humor comes when the audience recognizes believable characters caught in an absurd or wacky situation who continue struggling to reestablish a sense of balance.

• Lastly, be helpful to your partner. Work together to create the most interesting and dramatic scene you can. Acting is a partnership, just as being a member of an athletic team requires all the players to contribute to the success of the team.

DUETS

BETWEEN THE LINES
by *James Still*

<u>CHARACTERS</u>

JENNY: Almost 18.
RAN: Her sister, 14.

TIME: The present.
PLACE: A bedroom.

AT RISE: *JENNY looks around the room, distracted. She packs a couple of suitcases, rolls up posters, chooses CDs. There's a knock on the door.*

JENNY. Yeah?
RAN *(off)*. Jenny? It's me...
JENNY. Hi, me. *(Continues packing. She looks over at the closed door.)* Ran? What are you doing?
RAN *(off)*. Nothing.
JENNY. Then stop spying on me and come in.
RAN. Okay.

(RAN comes in the room, plops on the bed.)

JENNY. Why are you being so weird?
RAN. I'm not being weird. And I wasn't spying.
JENNY. Okay.
RAN. What are you doing?

JENNY. What does it look like I'm doing? I'm packing.

RAN. Oh.

JENNY. And I don't need any help, because I'm almost finished.

RAN. That's good, because I wasn't planning on helping. *(Beat.)* Are you nervous?

JENNY. No. Are you?

RAN. Why should I be nervous? You're the one who's leaving. I'm the one who's staying.

JENNY. Maybe that's why you're nervous.

RAN. I'm not nervous.

JENNY. Then stop tapping your foot.

(RAN looks at her foot unconsciously tapping the floor. She stops tapping.)

Think you're going to miss me? *(RAN doesn't answer. JENNY looks at her, smiles, lets it pass.)* I found a book that was due six months ago. It was under my bed next to a piece of pizza that looked like a dead animal.

RAN. Gross.

JENNY. It still tasted pretty good.

(RAN looks at JENNY, horrified. JENNY laughs loud.)

Gotcha. *(Beat.)*

RAN. What do you think it'll be like?

JENNY. What?

RAN. College.

JENNY. How should I know? I've never been to college.

(RAN starts tapping her foot again. JENNY walks over and puts her hand on her foot to stop it from tapping.)

It'll probably be like high school—only harder.

RAN. And more fun.

JENNY. Hopefully.

RAN. What if you don't like your roommate?

JENNY. I don't know. But after sharing this room with you for most of my life, I think I'm ready for anything.

RAN. Am I really that bad?

JENNY. The best.

RAN. The best?

JENNY. The best at being bad.

RAN. The best at being bad. I like that. *(Beat.)* Remember when I brought that tarantula home?

JENNY. The one you named "Kevin"?

RAN. Right. He just looked like a Kevin, you know?

JENNY. He just looked like a big, hairy, poisonous spider, you know?

RAN. Kinda like that guy you had a crush on in tenth grade. *(Beat.)* I'm not going to miss you, Jenny. But if I did, it would be awful. I mean, what if you left and I felt really really bad and I couldn't stand the idea of not sharing a room with you, of not talking to you late at night when Mom and Dad thought we were asleep... of not having somebody... *(Her voice trails off.)*

JENNY. Come on, Ran, how many times have you wished you could have this room all to yourself?

RAN. Six thousand two hundred and eight-six times. At least.

JENNY. Well... careful what you wish for.

RAN. Remember when you used to lock me out—

JENNY. And you'd climb on the roof—

RAN. And come in through the window—

JENNY. Wearing a mask that looked like the pope.

RAN. I think I had green hair then too.

JENNY. Oh yeah—Ran's Green Hair.

RAN. I liked it.

JENNY. I know you did. But sometimes I'd wake up in the middle of the night because a bright light was shining in my eyes. Only it turned out to be your neon green hair glowing in the dark.

RAN. My green hair glowed in the dark? Cool. *(Beat.)* Maybe I'll paint the walls black. After you're gone.

JENNY. Why?

RAN. Why not?

(JENNY laughs.)

What's so funny?

JENNY. We're really different, you know?

RAN. Remember when you had me convinced that I was adopted?

JENNY. It was a joke!

RAN. I know, but I believed you. And so I started asking everybody in town if they knew who my real parents were. I went right up to the Methodist minister and said, "Are you my father?"

JENNY. I thought Mom was going to die of embarrassment.

RAN. Well, they never had the blood tests. Who knows? Maybe it's true.

JENNY. No way. You're definitely my sister.

RAN. Why?

JENNY. I don't know. It's just something you know. It's something you can feel. It's like you share something— even though you don't know what it is. It's just something inside, you know? Something that feels... connected.

RAN. Connected to what?

JENNY. Ran!

RAN. I'm just trying to understand what you're talking about.

JENNY. Forget it.

RAN. Are you mad at me?

JENNY. Do you want me to be?

RAN. What is that supposed to mean?

JENNY. Oh come on, Ran. You always act so tough, it's like you're daring me to be mean or something. And now I'm moving away and going to college—and I think you want me to be mean so you can be mad at me.

RAN. Whatever.

JENNY. Because it's a lot easier not to miss somebody if you're mad at them.

RAN *(angry)*. I am not mad at you!

JENNY *(stares at RAN)*. Okay. *(Picks up an old stuffed animal and looks at it tenderly.)* Do you want this?

RAN. You don't want it?

JENNY. There's not enough room.

RAN. I don't really want it.

JENNY. I thought you liked it.

RAN. I used to. When I was like, six. *(A horn honks off-stage.)*

JENNY. I guess Dad is ready to go.

RAN. Either that or he's just checking to make sure the horn still works. *(Beat.)*

JENNY. You could still come, you know.

RAN *(thinks about it)*. No. It's your day. Besides, I hate it when Mom cries.

JENNY. Do you think she's going to cry?

RAN. Duh. I heard her crying last night. She's going to really really miss you. *(Beat.)*

JENNY. So.

RAN. So this is it. You're shipping out. College girl.

JENNY. Woman.

RAN. Whatever.

JENNY (taking a look around the room). Are you really going to paint the room black after I'm gone?

RAN. No.

JENNY. Good.

RAN. I'm going to paint it hot pink. With psychedelic murals on every wall. And on the ceiling, I'm going to paint the solar system. All the planets and all the moons and all the stars. And if I'm in the mood, I'll paint some extra planets and give them names like "Popcorn" and "Secrets" and... "Jenny."

JENNY. Okay.

(She reaches out to give RAN a hug and RAN slips away and starts circling JENNY.)

What are you doing?

RAN. I'm a moon. Orbiting around Planet Jenny. I'm an asteroid!

(She crashes into JENNY and manages to turn it into an awkward hug. RAN doesn't want to let go.)

JENNY. You're a nut.

RAN. Does that mean you're not going to go?

JENNY. Ran...

RAN. You could stay. I could bring you food, you could write all my papers and do my homework for me. I'll keep my side of the room spotless...

(The horn honks again. RAN finally lets go of JENNY. JENNY picks up the stuffed animal and gives it to RAN.)

JENNY. Look after him for me. *(To the stuffed animal.)* You're going to miss me, aren't you? I hope somebody does.

(She grabs her suitcases and exits the room. RAN cradles the animal.)

RAN *(to herself)*. Somebody does.

BLACKOUT

FRIENDS FOREVER
by Nancy Hanna

CHARACTERS

DUFFY: A high-flying risk-taker.

KELEY: Duffy's best friend. An excellent student who never causes trouble.

Note: Duffy may be played by a boy or girl.

TIME: The present.
PLACE: A rock bluff.

AT RISE: *DUFFY tries to get KELEY to jump off a rock into the river.*

DUFFY. So, explain it to me, would ya?
KELEY. I can't explain it. I'm just not ready for this.
DUFFY. Are you kidding? I've been waiting for this all my life.
KELEY. Your *whole* life? Wow, really?
DUFFY. Keley, don't jerk with me, okay? Just for one bright, clear moment, do something dangerous...exciting...spontaneous. You won't regret it, I promise.
KELEY. Sometimes, I regret the day I ever met you.
DUFFY. What's that supposed to mean?

KELEY. It's just you're always pushing me ... pushing me to places I don't want to go, into things I don't want to do. I was a good person before I met you, and now, sometimes I wonder. I've always tried to do what's right, please everyone ... my parents, teachers. And you, always asking me to take some kind of risk. We could get in trouble for this.

DUFFY. Keley, that's why we're so good for each other. We balance each other out. My grades have gone from C's to B's because of you.

KELEY. My grades have gone from high A's to low A's, and in science, I might even get a B.

DUFFY. Come on, admit it, you were boring before you met me. Now you laugh more ... you're happy. I've even heard you giggle.

KELEY. I did not giggle. I would not call it a giggle. I'm not that kind of girl, okay?

DUFFY. Giggling's good, it's like hot chocolate boiling over on the stove. You lose control, bubble over.

KELEY. That's stupid. I'm not like that. I don't want to be like that. You have a bad effect on me.

DUFFY. Come on, close your eyes. Hold my hand. *(Takes her hand.)* We're jumping on the count of three. One, two ...

KELEY. No. Stop. I won't. I don't want to jump off this rock into the river. It's dangerous. I'm not a good swimmer. We don't even have our bathing suits on. My shoes will get ruined. You're crazy. I've had it with you. I don't want to be friends anymore. Well, I don't mean that exactly. I mean, we can still say "hi" to each other in the hall. It's not like we won't speak to each other.

DUFFY. You're my only friend. Who'll laugh at my jokes? Who'll help me put soap in the park fountain at midnight and catch bubble clouds?

KELEY. That's the very thing I'm talking about. My parents would kill me if they knew I had anything to do with that.

DUFFY. It was fun. We covered you with bubbles—the abominable snow girl. You laughed till you wet your pants.

KELEY. I did not! And then you jumped in the fountain and threatened to eat all the gold fish.

DUFFY. I wasn't really going to eat them. I just like trying to catch the slimy, wiggly things.

KELEY. Then you came out and gave me a big wet, smelly hug. I was soaking wet.

DUFFY. You loved it.

KELEY. I was scared to death...a soggy, nervous wreck. And now you want us to jump off this rock into the river. It's too much for me...you're too much.

DUFFY. Okay, I'll just jump alone then, and you can watch me and applaud.

KELEY. But why? Why do you always want to do stuff like this? Scary stuff, where you could get hurt or get in trouble? What's so bad about *normal* life? Normal people don't jump in the river with their clothes on.

DUFFY. See that hawk, Keley? I'm like that hawk. I just want to fly a little higher, soar a little further. I like to perch on the end of branches. I'm not crazy. It's not like I want to die or anything. Lots of kids jump off this rock.

KELEY. You've been my best friend this year. Nobody gets how we could be friends. But if you're a hawk,

I'm a rabbit. I like to hop around fields in the early morning ... when the fog's still settling on the grass ... and it's quiet and green and moist on my toes. I like it calm and quiet.

DUFFY. A rabbit?

KELEY. A hawk?

DUFFY. Can a rabbit and a hawk be friends?

KELEY. I don't know.

DUFFY. Okay, Keley, you don't have to do anything you don't want to, but will the rabbit watch the hawk take flight? 'Cause I was born for flying.

KELEY. At least take your shoes off.

DUFFY. Okay. *(Removes shoes.)*

KELEY. Do you have any stuff in your pockets?

DUFFY. Here, hold my keys.

KELEY. Your glasses.

DUFFY *(hands her the glasses)*. Such an embarrassment, that a hawk should have to wear glasses. Here I go. Promise to applaud.

KELEY. Okay. Yes, definitely.

DUFFY. Here I go. Friends foreverrrrrr. *(Actor jumps in place, falls to fetal position.)*

KELEY. Look at you, you're flying, flying. *(Winces as DUFFY hits water.)* Friends forever.

BLACKOUT

WAITING FOR THE PHONE
by *Mark Plaiss*

CHARACTERS

MEEMEE: A teenager.
MOOMOO: A teenager.

TIME: The present.
PLACE: Anywhere.

I

(Lights come up to reveal MEEMEE and MOOMOO in chairs facing the audience. MEEMEE is sitting up very straight in a wooden straight-back chair, looking through a Viewmaster. He makes no movement except for his finger switching the slides. MOOMOO is slouched down in a soft, easy chair with his legs crossed reading a newspaper which is spread out on his lap. He is eating Chinese food from a carton with chopsticks, and wearing headphones. Between them is a small table on which rests a telephone. Fifteen to twenty seconds after the lights come up, the phone begins ringing. Neither of them makes any effort to answer it. They act as if they don't hear it. MEEMEE continues to look through his Viewmaster, and MOOMOO continues to eat, read, and listen to the music through his headphones. MOOMOO wipes his mouth

with a napkin. The phone rings for at least fifteen seconds. Finally, MEEMEE removes the Viewmaster from his eyes and snaps his head toward MOOMOO. Only his head moves, not his shoulders. And the move must be quick. MEEMEE stares at MOOMOO for a moment, then in a very exaggerated move, rears back and throws the Viewmaster at MOOMOO, striking him. MOOMOO turns to MEEMEE, not the least bit angered at being struck. MOOMOO removes the earphones and looks at the telephone a moment. Then he picks up.)

MOOMOO *(after listening a moment).* You've got the wrong number. *(Lights go out immediately.)*

II

(Lights come up to reveal MEEMEE and MOOMOO in same chairs, facing audience. They are now old men. MEEMEE is blind and is wearing dark glasses. He is sitting up very straight. He doesn't move a muscle. In his lap he holds a white red-tipped cane that blind people use. MOOMOO is once again slouched down in the easy chair eating Chinese food from a carton, this time with a fork. He's reading a newspaper which is spread out across his legs. A huge hearing aid, the old-fashioned horn kind, rests on the floor and reaches right up against his ear. Thirty seconds after the lights come up, the phone begins ringing. MEEMEE remains perfectly stiff, and MOOMOO continues reading and eating. The phone rings for at least fifteen seconds. Finally, MEEMEE snaps his head toward MOOMOO. Only his head

moves. He looks at MOOMOO a moment. Then, without moving anything but his wrist, MEEMEE whacks MOOMOO with his cane. MOOMOO looks at MEEMEE not the least bit angry for being struck. He looks down at the ringing phone. He picks up the phone, listens a moment, then hangs up. He returns to eating and reading. All this time MEEMEE continues to have his head turned to MOOMOO. MEEMEE doesn't move a muscle.)

MEEMEE *(loudly)*. And?

MOOMOO *(loudly, without looking up from paper)*. She said she'd call back tomorrow. *(Lights fade.)*

BLACKOUT

RUNAWAY
by Jett Parsley

CHARACTERS

LEE: Age 16.
R.C.: A trucker, about 30.

TIME: The present.
PLACE: A truck stop in North Carolina.

AT RISE: *LEE enters and rests a bit, leaning against R.C.'s truck. After a moment, R.C. enters and sees her.*

R.C. That's my truck you're leanin' against, girl.
LEE. *Your* truck? *(She checks him over.)* Lucky me.
R.C. Come on. Move it. I gotta hit the road. *(She doesn't move.)*
LEE. That's a mighty big truck.
R.C. I'm carrying a mighty big load of mighty big TV sets.
LEE. Where you headed?
R.C. New York.
LEE. What a coincidence. I need a ride to New York.
R.C. *(pause, looking her over).* What if I said I was goin' to D.C.?
LEE. Then I'd say I was goin' to D.C.
R.C. *(pause).* No way. Git.
(LEE moves up close to him, runs a hand up his arm.)

17

LEE. Move where?

R.C. *(pulls away)*. Back where you came from. I don't give rides.

LEE. I can pay you.

R.C. I don't want your *payment.*

LEE. Money.

R.C. No thanks.

LEE. Come on, mister—

R.C. How old are you?

LEE. What do you care?

R.C. I care 'cause I ain't gettin' picked up the minute I cross the border for transporting some fifteen-year-old hooker—

LEE. First of all I'm *not* a hooker, and second of all I'm *nineteen*, so you don't have to—

R.C. Nineteen?

LEE. Yeah.

R.C. Show me some I.D.

LEE. I don't drive. That's why I need the ride.

R.C. Right. Beat it.

LEE. New York's not but—what—ten hours from here? I'll sit in the trailer. You'll never know I was around.

R.C. I can't have some person I don't know back there with those TVs. You could steal somethin' or damage it.

LEE *(pause, then soft)*. Mister.

R.C. You heard me.

LEE. Mister, I got to get out of here.

(Something in her voice catches him. He takes a deeper look at her.)

You can just take me up the road to the next town and drop me off. I'll find another ride. But I got to get out of this town. Today.

R.C. Ain't there someone who's gonna miss you?

LEE. No.

R.C. How about school?

LEE. I told you, I'm nineteen. I'm not in school. I was workin' at the Quik Stop but I got in a fight with the manager—

R.C. Who would be...

LEE *(pause; knows he's trying to trick her)*. Bobbi Ann. You know her?

R.C. *(pause)*. Go on.

LEE. Anyway, I got in a fight with her 'bout this guy and so now I've got no job and no reason to stay in this old place. *(He doesn't answer.)* Look, okay, that guy Bobbi Ann and I were fightin' about, well, he's mad at me, too, and...he gets kinda mean. *(She slips up a sleeve and shows a bruise on her arm.)*

R.C. *(pause)*. You got any stuff?

LEE. Got a suitcase 'round the corner. I'll go get it. *(She disappears for a moment, returns with a suitcase.)* It's not too big, is it?

R.C. *(angry, probably at himself)*. No.

LEE. Well, let's go.

R.C. Yeah. *(He puts her suitcase in the truck.)*

LEE. So where *are* we goin'?

R.C. New York.

LEE. Great. What's your name?

R.C. R.C. Like the cola. What's yours?

LEE *(pause)*. Lee. Like the general.

R.C. Always in charge.

LEE. Exactly.

BLACKOUT

THE DROPOUT
by *John O'Brien*

CHARACTERS

STUDENT
TEACHER

TIME: The present.
PLACE: A classroom.

AT RISE: *A TEACHER sits alone at her desk. A STU-DENT enters.*

STUDENT. Excuse me.
TEACHER. There's nothing to excuse. My door is always open.
STUDENT. It was closed.
TEACHER. I was speaking figuratively.
STUDENT. Excuse me?
TEACHER. I'm sorry. I shouldn't have tried to communicate. State your business.
STUDENT. I don't getchou.
TEACHER. "I gotta use words when I talk to you." That's from T.S. Eliot.
STUDENT. My name's not Eliot.
TEACHER. Let's get this over with. What do you want?
STUDENT *(handing the TEACHER a form in triplicate).* You gotta sign this.

TEACHER. I do?

STUDENT. On the bottom.

TEACHER. Who says I have to sign it?

STUDENT. My guidance counselor.

TEACHER. Which one?

STUDENT. The guy wid glasses.

TEACHER. I don't mean to discombobulate you, but there are *two* guys with glasses in the guidance department.

STUDENT. The guy wid glasses and a bald head.

TEACHER. Let me get this straight. Your guidance counselor, the guy with glasses and a bald head, says that I must sign this form on the bottom, in triplicate.

STUDENT. Yup.

TEACHER. I'm glad that's settled. Do you have a pen?

STUDENT. No.

TEACHER. What a surprise. A pencil?

STUDENT. No.

TEACHER. I'm astonished. You call yourself a student, but you have neither pen nor pencil.

STUDENT. If you sign that, I won't be a student no more.

TEACHER. It looks to me as though you never were. *(Puts the form aside.)*

STUDENT. Ain'tcha gonna sign it?

TEACHER. Tomorrow, if time permits.

STUDENT. I need it now.

TEACHER. Do you?

STUDENT. Please sign it.

TEACHER. Did you say please?

STUDENT. Yes.

TEACHER. That's different from, "You gotta sign it."

STUDENT. I hafta show it to my udder teachas.

TEACHER. Your *udder* teachers?

STUDENT. Before they go home.

TEACHER. Did you ever milk a cow?

STUDENT. No.

TEACHER. Do you know what a cow is?

STUDENT. Yes.

TEACHER. Is it animal, mineral, or vegetable?

STUDENT. Animal.

TEACHER. Is it bigger than a breadbox?

STUDENT. I don't know.

TEACHER. You never saw a breadbox?

STUDENT. Please sign it.

TEACHER. So you can show it to your *udder* teachers?

STUDENT. Yes.

TEACHER. I might as well. Why fight it? What is it anyway?

STUDENT. It's so's I can quit school.

TEACHER. Quit? When did you join?

STUDENT. This says I don't owe you no books.

TEACHER. I can read what it says.

STUDENT. That's my name there.

TEACHER. And whose name, pray tell, is this?

STUDENT. My father.

TEACHER. Your father's name and your name are not the same name.

STUDENT. He's my stepfather.

TEACHER (*playing Sherlock Holmes*). What's this? What's this? I say, Watson, old chap, what do you make of this? Do you recognize this name?

STUDENT. That's you.

TEACHER. Me? Why would my name and your name be on the same form?

STUDENT. I got you for English.

TEACHER. So it says here, but the year is half over, and I've never seen you.

STUDENT. I seen you.

TEACHER. Have you really?

STUDENT. On the first day of school.

TEACHER. And you haven't been back since?

STUDENT. Here's the book.

TEACHER. What book?

STUDENT. The one you give me on the first day.

TEACHER *(putting a piece of paper over the book)*. Who wrote it?

STUDENT. I don't know.

TEACHER. What's the title?

STUDENT. I don't know.

TEACHER. Did you ever read a book?

STUDENT. No.

TEACHER. Why do you call yourself a student?

STUDENT. Please sign it. I give you the book.

TEACHER. I'll sign it if you promise never to come back to my class.

STUDENT. I promise.

TEACHER *(starting to sign the form)*. Where have you been since the first day?

STUDENT. I don't wanta say.

TEACHER. Maybe I don't want to sign.

STUDENT. My mother tried to kill herself.

TEACHER *(signs form and hands it to the STUDENT)*. She tried and failed?

STUDENT. She's been in a coma

TEACHER. Since the first day of school?

STUDENT. Yes.

TEACHER. Why are you quitting now?

STUDENT. She died today.

TEACHER. Why quit school?

STUDENT. I gotta move out.

TEACHER. Of your home?

STUDENT. I ain't got no home. My stepfather don't want me around.

TEACHER. Here. Keep the book.

STUDENT. I don't read books.

TEACHER. Maybe you will someday.

STUDENT. Thanks.

TEACHER. Sorry for the sarcasm. It's an occupational hazard.

STUDENT. That's okay.

TEACHER. No, it's not.

STUDENT. We all got problems. *(Exits.)*

TEACHER. You're telling me.

BLACKOUT

MIMI AND THE MONSTER
by Jett Parsley

CHARACTERS

MIMI: An adult librarian who lives alone.

MONSTER: Comes from under her bed. Played by a male. He is dressed in black, face painted or wears a mask.

TIME: The present.
PLACE: Mimi's bedroom.

AT RISE: *MIMI dashes into the room, dives onto the bed, squirrels away under the covers, a small, huddled, hidden creature. Pause. Slowly she peeks out, then hides again.*

MIMI *(quickly).* Go away! Go away! Go away! *(Silence. Slowly, her hand comes out, feeling around until it rests on a teddy bear, which she snatches and pulls under the covers with her.)* You look, Pookie. ...What? *You're* not *afraid*... But somebody has to look, and you're so strong. And besides, monsters don't eat teddy bears. ...OK. Good. *(The hand and bear return. The bear moves slowly to the edge of the bed, then over the side. It "looks" underneath, returns under the covers.)* Nothing there? *(MIMI and bear emerge.)* Are you *sure?* *(The bear "nods.")* Well. Well, then. Maybe I'll just look myself. Just a quick look. Since nothing's there. Nothing scary at all. *(Very slowly, MIMI stretches out so that she can lean just her head off the bed to check under. She suddenly screams and flees backward, under the covers.)* Oh, my God!

(A MONSTER slides out from under the bed.)

MIMI. Oh, oh, go away! Oh no! Oh no, Oh, go away. *(She disappears under the covers.)* I'm dreaming—I've got to be dreaming! *(She peaks out then hides again.)* You're still here! Oh, what do you want? *(He slides the covers off her face.)* Don't! *(She tugs at the covers. He tugs back.)* Quit it, Stop that! Don't! *(She slaps at his hands and he pulls back.)* Oh! I didn't mean... I'm sorry. Did I hurt you? What am I saying? Take that, you...! I'm pretty strong—and mean—so don't get any ideas about...anything...see? *(She looks at him. He looks at her.)* What are you? *(Silence.)* So...do something. Make the first move. Come on. *(He comes closer, puts his face close to hers, studying.)* What... hey, not too... *(He continues to stare at her, then:)*
MONSTER. Your eyes are blue.

(She gasps. It is her turn to be speechless.)

I've never seen them open.

(A long moment while they stare at each other.)
MIMI *(timid again)*. Please go away.
MONSTER. I don't want to hurt you.
MIMI. Please...
MONSTER. I've just come out for this one time.
MIMI. What...what do you mean?
MONSTER *(pause)*. I thought you'd be much braver.

MIMI. Who's not brave? *(She reaches out and pokes him quickly, then pulls back, gathers her nerves.)* I—I can't believe—and you're—but, it's not supposed to be *real*, the monster under the bed; it's just something you think about as a child, but you know ... it's not *real* ...

MONSTER. Then why did you check?

MIMI. I check every night.

MONSTER. I know.

MIMI. You came from under my bed. You actually came from under my bed. There are actually monsters living under my bed.

MONSTER. Does that bother you?

MIMI. Are there monsters in the closet, too?

MONSTER. Monsters in the closet. Don't be ridiculous.

MIMI. Well, you can't stay. This is *my* bed, my room. Out. Or, under. Back from whence you came, and all that. *(He doesn't move.)* Come on, now! Out! Go! *(Nothing.)* I can't sleep with you there.

MONSTER. You've always slept with me there.

MIMI. I didn't *know* you were there.

MONSTER. Now you do.

MIMI *(pause)*. Are you a good monster or a bad monster?

MONSTER. That depends.

MIMI. Oh what?

MONSTER. Whether I ate dinner. Whether the night-light is on. Whether I like you.

MIMI *(pause)*. No, no, I'm sorry, but you're going to have to leave. This will never work. Pookie is afraid.

MONSTER. Monsters don't eat teddy bears. Barbie dolls, yes.

MIMI. Is that supposed to make me feel better?

MONSTER. Don't be afraid.

MIMI. That's easy for you to say. I don't even know your name.

MONSTER. You couldn't pronounce it. It is not a human language.

MIMI. What's under the mask?

MONSTER. There is nothing under the mask.

MIMI. That's it. Out! You *have* to go now. You *have* to!

MONSTER. I can't. I've watched you for too long. At night. When you were a child.

MIMI. You knew me then? You followed me?

MONSTER. There are tunnels. I can go anywhere, under any bed.

MIMI. Really?

MONSTER. You had a canopy bed with a pink canopy and ruffles.

MIMI. Yes.

MONSTER. At your grandmother's house the bed was very large, and you slept with your brother and sister.

MIMI *(pause)*. We had grand pillow fights. *(Pause.)* Oh, I don't know what to think of all this. *(Pause.)* These tunnels. Could you go anywhere, really?

MONSTER. Mmmm.

MIMI. But you came *here*? You followed *me*?

MONSTER *(pause)*. You tell stories.

MIMI. Stories? I don't know any stories.

MONSTER. Maybe they are your dreams. They are about many things, mermaids and ocelots and men who drink rum. You whisper them. I have to get very close to hear. Lie beside you and put my ear next to your mouth. This has happened all your life.

MIMI. *I* do that?

MONSTER. Yes.

MIMI. No.

MONSTER. Yes.

MIMI. No one ever told me.

MONSTER. You do not do it with anyone else. Only when you are alone.

MIMI. Which is most of the time. *(Pause.)* Only I wasn't really alone.

MONSTER. No.

MIMI *(pause)*. What's under your mask?

MONSTER. Nothing.

MIMI. You just don't want me to see.

MONSTER. You don't want to see.

MIMI *(pause)*. What's under the bed?

MONSTER. Many amazing things.

MIMI. Tunnels, you said.

MONSTER. And rivers. And forests.

MIMI. Forests? *(Pause.)* Can a... can a human person go there?

MONSTER. I don't think a human person would want to go there.

MIMI. Why not? Is it scary?

MONSTER. Sometimes.

MIMI. Oh.

MONSTER. What do you do in the day?

MIMI. I work the reference desk in a library. Sometimes I shelve books.

MONSTER. Do you find your stories there?

MIMI. I really don't know these stories you're talking about. Ask the fellows in the library. There's just nothing very creative about me at all.

MONSTER. I don't understand. The reason I came out tonight, the reason I entered your waking time, was because of the stories.

MIMI. Can't you make up your own stories?

MONSTER. Impossible. We monsters have no...what is
the human word...imagination.

MIMI. No imagination? Is that true?

MONSTER. We cannot lie, also.

MIMI. Must be pretty dull to be a monster.

MONSTER. Not if you know the tunnels. Not if you know
where the stories are to be found. Only now you say
you don't know them.

MIMI. I don't!

MONSTER. I thought that you must have more, I thought
you would tell them.

MIMI. Well, I guess you thought wrong.

MONSTER. I thought that someone who tells such stories
in her *sleep*...that with her eyes open she might be...
someone magic.

MIMI. I'm sorry...to disappoint.

MONSTER. You don't know what a treasure your stories
are.

MIMI. No one has ever said anything I had was a treasure.
(Pause.) Take me under the bed.

MONSTER. What? Impossible.

MIMI. No one will miss me.

MONSTER. It can't be done. A human has never entered
that world.

MIMI. No human ever knew that world existed!

MONSTER. I wanted to come out, you know...before.
But there are rules.

MIMI. Are you breaking a rule tonight?

MONSTER. Yes.

MIMI. Can you get in trouble?

MONSTER. I would get in more trouble for taking you under.

MIMI. But you will.

MONSTER. I don't understand why you—

MIMI. I'm curious.

MONSTER. You want to leave this world.

MIMI. Nothing for me here but a TV that only gets three stations and a landlady that won't get rid of the mice in my kitchen.

MONSTER. You already have a place of escape. Your stories.

MIMI. I keep telling you I don't know them.

MONSTER *(pause)*. I will tell you one.

MIMI. What? Why?

MONSTER. I will tell you one and then you'll remember.

MIMI. I doubt it.

MONSTER. Then I suppose I will ... just ... go back into the tunnel.

MIMI. Well, I ... I didn't say I ...

MONSTER. They are like a journey under the bed, an adventure to somewhere fantastical.

MIMI. I can't believe they're all *that* wonderful.

MONSTER. Once upon a time—

MIMI. Wait, wait, don't start yet. *(She settles into the bed.)* OK. Ready.

BLACKOUT

LUCK
by *Laura Shamas*

CHARACTERS

RACHEL: Age 15.
MARNIE: Also 15.

TIME: The present.
PLACE: A bus stop.

AT RISE: *Lights fade up on RACHEL and MARNIE, casually dressed, holding textbooks and waiting for a bus. They are standing on a big patch of green carpet or astroturf, representing grass. A bench is nearby. RACHEL chews gum and checks her watch impatiently. MARNIE puts her books down and starts staring intensely at the patch of greenery. She squats down, staring, her back to RACHEL and the audience. RACHEL looks at MARNIE with concern. RACHEL takes out her gum and disposes of it.*

RACHEL. The bus sure is late.
MARNIE *(from her squatting position)*. Uh-huh.
RACHEL. Hey, are you all right? You lose something?
MARNIE. I'm fine, thanks. *(She keeps staring intently at the ground, moving her fingers through the patch of greenery.)*
RACHEL *(a beat)*. You feeling okay?

MARNIE. Yeah, thanks.

RACHEL. Sure. *(A pause while RACHEL tries to act non-chalant. She turns around and watches MARNIE.)* You sure you didn't drop a contact or something?

MARNIE *(looking up)*. No. I'm fine, really.

RACHEL *(putting down her books)*. I got it. You're practicing yoga or t'ai chi.

MARNIE. No. No. I'm looking for something.

RACHEL *(crossing to her)*. I asked you that. Want some help?

MARNIE. No. I didn't lose anything. But I'm looking for something. You can look if you want. I won't stop you.

RACHEL. Hey, if someone offers help, you're supposed to be friendly back.

MARNIE. Look, I don't know you. I've seen you in the halls. I appreciate that you're trying to be nice. But I don't need any help.

RACHEL. You said you were looking for something.

MARNIE *(standing up)*. Okay. Okay. If you must know. I'm looking for four-leaf clovers.

RACHEL. What?

MARNIE. Four-leaf clovers.

RACHEL *(laughing)*. No one looks for four-leaf clovers anymore.

MARNIE *(moves to another side of patch)*. So. I'm the oldest person looking. Better odds for me. I need the luck today.

RACHEL *(still laughing)*. There's no such thing as four-leaf clovers.

MARNIE. Oh yes there are. There's one in every patch. I've found hundreds of them. I had a huge collection in fifth grade. It's an ancient tradition dating back to the

Druids. My parents taught me how to look. Hey, you know. There are five- and six-leafers, too. Once I even found a seven-leafer.

RACHEL *(quietly, inching away from her)*. So you're some kind of leaf freak?

MARNIE. No.

RACHEL. Maybe you could get on a talk show.

MARNIE. Make fun of it if you want. But all my life I've had pretty good luck.

RACHEL *(sits on bench)*. You probably like science classes.

MARNIE. Yes. As a matter of fact.

RACHEL. Um, what's your name?

MARNIE. Marnie.

RACHEL. I'm Rachel. Take a leaf break for a minute, Marnie.

MARNIE. Okay. *(She sits on bench by RACHEL.)*

RACHEL. Look, Marnie. Luck doesn't depend on a silly charm. That's stupid. We all make our own luck. By our actions.

MARNIE. How do you know that?

RACHEL. Well, let's say I want something to go well. I do my best. That's all the control I have. That's all I can do. It's not going to be any better if I carry around a piece of mutating clover. That's illogical.

MARNIE. I disagree. You *have* to do your best, all the time, sure. Obviously. But there is magic in life, too, things we can't explain. It's always there, too.

RACHEL. You're talking about God, right?

MARNIE. Not just God. Some things in life just aren't logical. Some things you just *know*, in your heart. And there are lots of things in life you can't prove. You can't find a rational category for everything. In fact, I think the best things in life are the surprises, the things you can't control, the little miracles.

RACHEL. Like what?

MARNIE *(standing)*. Like what really causes balled lightning. Or what makes cut grass smell so good in the summertime. Or what makes salmon swim upstream in the fall. Or why two people fall in love. That can't be explained. And there's luck involved.

RACHEL *(also standing)*. Now you're talking fate.

MARNIE. No. Fate is your destiny no matter what. Luck is knowing that something *good* will happen. Fate is not always good.

RACHEL. That's true. You ever been in love?

MARNIE. I don't know. One guy told me he loved me. Once.

RACHEL. Lots of guys say so. Did *you* feel it? Did *you* feel you loved him?

MARNIE. I thought so for the first few months. Then, well...I don't want to talk about it. We broke up.

RACHEL *(sighing)*. I want to fall in love someday.

MARNIE *(kneels down, picks something)*. Aha! You want a four-leaf clover?

(She holds it up. RACHEL crouches to see it.)

RACHEL. Cool! You really found one! It's so pretty! *(They stand up.)*

MARNIE. You can have it.

RACHEL. Really?

MARNIE. Sure. Maybe it'll help you fall in love. It'll bring you good luck.

RACHEL. You said you needed luck today.

MARNIE. Yeah, I do. But that's okay.

RACHEL. Why do you need luck?

MARNIE *(quietly).* I have a job interview. Part-time. I—we—my family—we really need the money. *(Looks at her watch.)* If the bus isn't here soon, I'm gonna miss my chance. *(A pause.)*

RACHEL. You take it. I give you all my luck today. I'll start looking for these four-leafers on my own.

MARNIE. You sure?

RACHEL. Yeah. I'll give you some competition. Now you won't be the oldest person looking anymore. Especially now that I know they really exist.

MARNIE. Maybe sometime we can look together. I'll teach you all my tips.

RACHEL. Great. Then I'll become a leaf freak, too!

MARNIE. We can design T-shirts that say "LEAF FREAK." *(The sounds of traffic are heard.)* I'm in luck. The bus is here. The four-leaf clover is working. *(They gather up their books.)*

RACHEL. I'm in luck, too. I think I found something, too.

MARNIE. What?

RACHEL. A friend.

(They smile.)

BLACKOUT

CUE TO CUE
by John O'Brien

CHARACTERS

GWEN: In her teens.
LOIS: Also in her teens.

The number of roles can be expanded.

TIME: The present.
PLACE: The street.

(The characters have fallen into the rut of using conversation as a ping-pong game.)

GWEN. Hi, Lois.
LOIS. Hi, Gwen.
GWEN. You look good.
LOIS. I feel good.
GWEN. You feel well.
LOIS. Excuse me?
GWEN. You look good. You feel well.
LOIS. What are you, sick?
GWEN. I'm not sick now, but I have been sick. I had chicken pox last month.
LOIS. My grandmother has a chicken. She lives in Minnesota.

37

GWEN. I had a soda last night. Freddie Henderson bought it for me. We sipped it together with two straws, just like they do in the old movies on TV.

LOIS. I love straw. My aunt has a straw mattress in her attic. Whenever we visit her, I get to sleep on it.

GWEN. I get to sleep about two o'clock every morning, especially when I have bad dreams.

LOIS. Isn't he a dream, that boy over there?

GWEN *(singing)*. "Over there, over there." That was a big song in WWI. I learned that in history.

LOIS. My history teacher is always absent. We had three different substitutes last week.

GWEN. I've been feeling weak lately. I may have mono. That's what my mother says.

LOIS. Mothers are a pain.

GWEN. I have a pain in my side. Every time I turn fast, I get a stitch.

LOIS. Did you ever see my appendix stitches? I think the doctor was drunk.

GWEN. My boyfriend got drunk last summer. I told him he had to choose: me or the booze. I haven't seen him since.

LOIS. I was a lifeguard last summer. All I did was sit in the chair and sleep. What a racket.

GWEN. I need a new racket. The strings broke on my old one.

LOIS. My boyfriend is stringing me along. So I said to him: "I don't mind playing second fiddle, but please don't string me along." He didn't get it.

GWEN. My cousin plays fiddle in the school orchestra.

LOIS. School is a waste.

GWEN. I have to watch my waist. I'm getting fat.

LOIS. I lost my watch in gym class.

GWEN. Have you seen Jim Ryan? What a doll.

LOIS. I got dolled up last week to go out with a guy I met.

GWEN. Have you seen Guy Carter? He's only a freshman, but he's out of this world.

LOIS. A man got fresh with me the other day on the subway.

GWEN. We had a sub yesterday in cooking.

LOIS. I love cooking.

GWEN. I love cookies, but I hate cake.

LOIS. Do you know Cookie Lambert? He's a space cadet.

GWEN. There's a big space next to our house, ever since the house that used to be there burned down.

LOIS. Do you know what burns me up? Chip Tanso got a B in English, and he don't know nuttin'.

GWEN. My father says I'm a chip off the old block.

LOIS. I used to hang around the old block, but I'm getting too old to hang around.

GWEN. I have a hang-up about a kid in my typing class.

LOIS. I went out with a boy last weekend, but he wasn't my type. One date was the beginning and the end.

GWEN. I'll be at the end of my rope if I don't meet somebody soon.

LOIS. "Give a man enough rope, and he'll hang himself." That's what my father says.

GWEN. Graduation seems farther away every day.

LOIS. I weigh more than I ever did before.

GWEN. Before I met Charley, I used to like Fred.

LOIS. My brother bought a used car last night.

GWEN. Fred was a knight in shining armor.

LOIS. Look at the sun shining on the sugar bowl.

GWEN. I went bowling Monday night.

LOIS. Mondays should be outlawed.

GWEN. Jesse James was an outlaw.

LOIS. My Uncle Jimmy's name is James.

GWEN. "A rose by any other name would smell as sweet."

LOIS. I was sweet on Eric until I met John.

GWEN. I gotta go to the john.

LOIS. I'm always on the go.

GWEN. Always is a long, long time. *(She exits.)*

LOIS. Distance equals rate times time. *(To the audience.)* I'll bet you didn't think I knew that.

BLACKOUT

BULLFROGS AND BISCUITS
by Nancy Hanna

CHARACTERS

ARLIE
EDIE

TIME: The present.
PLACE: Near Caddo Lake,
on the border of Texas and Louisiana.

ARLIE loves EDIE and comes to visit her. They discuss their possible relationship knowing Edie's father will never approve.

AT RISE: *ARLIE watches EDIE from the porch. Enters, sneaks up behind her and puts his hands over her eyes. She jumps.*

ARLIE *(referring to Edie's father).* Ugly's out fishin' about a mile down the lake.

EDIE *(jumps up, alarmed).* Arlie Ford, what are you doing here? How did you find me all the way out here? What do you think yer doin'? You've got to get outta here, right now.

ARLIE. It took some doin', I must say. I never even seen this part of Caddo, an' one time or another, I've been all over this lake.

41

EDIE. Arlie Ford, please leave. You don't know my daddy. An' you don't want to know him.

ARLIE. It'll take him some time to paddle his boat back up here. He's gnarly, idn't he?

EDIE. Yeah. *(Giving in.)* So you have five minutes.

ARLIE. I knew you'd like me bein' around.

EDIE. You're not bad—for a bullfrog, that is.

ARLIE. I'm not a bullfrog.

EDIE. According to Aunt June you are. All boys are.

ARLIE. Well, I'm not a "boy" now, am I?

EDIE. You look like a boy to me. And if you're not, what are ya?

ARLIE. I'm a man.

EDIE. And I'm Spanish moss, blowin' with the breeze.

ARLIE. Is this a riddle?

EDIE. No. It's Aunt June's idea of men and women, boys and girls...you know, relating.

ARLIE. Now this is gettin' interesting. So, according to June, I'm a bullfrog and yer Spanish moss?

EDIE. Blowin' in the breeze. And that's all I'm gonna say about that.

ARLIE. If boys are bullfrogs, I thought girls would be lily pads.

EDIE *(scolding).* Arlie Ford—if you want to know more, about bullfrogs and Spanish moss, you'll have to ask Aunt June. Second thought, don't go anywhere near her. She's taken to some dangerous thinkin'.

ARLIE. What do frogs and moss have in common? Edie, I'm gonna get to the bottom of this. Yer gonna tell me everything, about me bein' a bullfrog and you bein' Spanish moss.

EDIE *(pushes him away).* I'm not telling you a thing.

ARLIE. What's this? *(Sees doll and picks it up.)*
EDIE *(embarrassed)*. Sally Mae. *(Takes the doll from him.)*
ARLIE. You still play with baby dolls?
EDIE. My mama gave her to me when I was just a baby. She's my best friend, so you best keep your manners around her. She's just about all I got in the world, Arlie.
ARLIE. I'll buy you a new doll, a dozen of 'em if you want.
EDIE. No, thank you. This one's just fine.
ARLIE. I'd do anything for you, Edie. You just say the word. Go ahead, tell her, Sally Mae, tell her I'm her knight in armor, come to take her away.
(EDIE makes the doll signify indifference.)
  Can I kiss you, Edie? Sally Mae thinks it would be a very good idea. Don't you, Sally Mae?
EDIE. No, she certainly does not. Do you, Sally Mae? *(She makes the doll's head shake no. EDIE rises.)* You better go. My daddy's gonna be here any minute. I got the newspaper, with his lotto numbers. You better go.
ARLIE. Yer gettin' older. He can't have you forever.
EDIE. I know that. I just don't think he knows that.
ARLIE. Would you like me to explain it to him?
EDIE. There's no explainin' nothin' to him, Arlie. There's just waitin'.
ARLIE. I'm good at the art of arguin', Edie. Just ask my daddy. I can be very persuasive.
EDIE. He's not like yer daddy. His kinda man settles things other ways... pushin' and forcin' what they want.
ARLIE. I think I love you.
EDIE. That's nice. I do appreciate it.

ARLIE. No, I mean really. I'm serious about you, Edie. Yer kind and strong. There's things about you, I've never seen in anyone else. Things you know, I want to know. You see, I want to see. Besides that, you're the prettiest girl in the county and I'm the handsomest guy. We go together like biscuits and gravy, black-eyed peas and New Year's Day.

EDIE. Stop it, will ya. Besides...all that talk of food's makin' me hungry. (She looks out the window.)

ARLIE (comes up behind her). That's just what I was hopin'. You do like me, don't you? Just a little?

EDIE. You don't know nothin' about what I see.

ARLIE. Give me a chance. That's all I'm askin'.

EDIE (turns toward him). I do like you.

(They touch their fingertips together.)

Just a little.

(Both looking at their hands touching.)

Might be just a little more than that.

(Looks up and sees her father out the window. Pushes ARLIE away.)

Lord Almighty, here he comes! It's Daddy. Come quick, this way.

(They move toward the bathroom.)

ARLIE. You do like me.

EDIE. Where'd you park? He better not have seen yer car.

ARLIE. More than a little, that's what I heard. I'm comin' to visit you tonight, Miss Edie Catz.

EDIE. Don't dare do that!

ARLIE. A proper visit, right here in front of old numb nut. He's got to see, you've got to have yer own life.

EDIE. That won't work. Don't come out here. He might hurt you. Do somethin' bad.

ARLIE. You're worried for my safety. That's a good sign.

EDIE. Come on, you got to get out o' the bathroom window.

ARLIE. You mean this place's got indoor plumbing?

EDIE *(pushing him)*. Now.

ARLIE *(takes her hand)*. I want to split open the night sky and get the moon for you, Edie. Catch a million fireflies and light up what's dark. I do, and I will. You wait and see.

EDIE *(looks out the window)*. God Almighty, here he comes. Come on. *(She pushes ARLIE offstage L.)* Out the window.

ARLIE *(offstage)*. I'm comin' to get you.

EDIE. Get outta here. And don't you dare come back.

ARLIE. I'm comin' tonight. We're gonna sit on the porch steps an' I'm gonna hold yer hand. Tell her to let me in, Sally Mae.

EDIE. Stop it. Don't come. Do you hear me?

ARLIE. See you around seven, Miss Edie Catz.

BLACKOUT

ICE CREAM & WAR STORIES
by *Allison Gregory*

CHARACTERS

EVEN STEVEN NGUYEN: An Asian-American boy, 10.
GRANDMA OLIVE: His Caucasian grandmother.

TIME: The present.
PLACE: Even's bedroom.

On the night before he moves away from the house his grandfather grew up in, EVEN STEVEN NGUYEN's longing to know his grandfather—who disappeared during the Vietnam War before EVEN was born—becomes more urgent. GRANDMA OLIVE has difficulty revealing to EVEN her true feelings about the war and EVEN's war-torn heritage.

AT RISE: *GRANDMA enters with a bowl of ice cream. EVEN is staring out the window.*

GRANDMA. Any UFOs?
EVEN. Funny, Grandma.
GRANDMA. I brought you some ice cream. Vanilla.
EVEN. I'm not hungry.
GRANDMA. You don't need to be hungry to eat ice cream. Oops. *(She spills some ice cream onto her shoe.)*

More for my shoe. *(Pause.)* You'd be surprised what you see if you stand at that window long enough.

EVEN. I've looked out this window a thousand times. I've never seen any UFOs.

GRANDMA. Maybe you weren't looking right. Were you just looking *out*, or did you look *inside out*?

EVEN. Inside out?

GRANDMA. Or backwards, or underneath?

EVEN. Underneath *what*?

GRANDMA. It's a perspective. You're only going to see things differently when you change the way you look. What have we got here? *(She stands next to him at the window.)*

EVEN. Just houses.

GRANDMA. Isn't that interesting.

EVEN. Not really.

GRANDMA *(looks sideways out the window)*. I see the Morales' house stacked onto the Rollins' house which is sitting on old man Meyer's house. Hope there's no strong winds tonight, the whole stack is liable to blow over. Do you see that cat?

EVEN *(bends sideways and looks out)*. It looks like it's hanging from the sidewalk!

(She bends further to the side, tilting her head until she is looking upside down. He does the same.)

GRANDMA. If it's not clever, it's going to drop right onto the stars.

EVEN. Look at the Morales' car in front of that big sycamore tree.

GRANDMA. The tree is BLOOMING the car. Fascinating.

EVEN. I don't want to move to a new house, Grandma. I like it here.

GRANDMA. You think that now. When we get settled in, you'll forget.

EVEN. I don't want to forget. Why do we have to leave?

GRANDMA. This house doesn't fit anymore. It's filled with too many memories.

EVEN. What if Grandpa comes back and we've moved away? *(Pause.)*

GRANDMA. I don't think he's coming back, E.

EVEN. But you don't know for sure. The government said he was "Unaccounted For." They just couldn't find him.

GRANDMA. That's what they—

EVEN. You said it was far away. *(He takes an atlas out of the book box and opens it to a marked page.)* You showed me on this map, here:

EVEN & GRANDMA *(simultaneously).* "Ten thousand miles across the ocean."

GRANDMA. That's right. But it's been a long time since the war.

EVEN. Maybe he got injured. Maybe he has *amnesia.* Maybe—

GRANDMA. Don't get your hopes wrong, E.

EVEN. But it's *possible*, isn't it?

GRANDMA. It's possible.

EVEN. What if he finally came home and we weren't here? Just strangers living in his house. He wouldn't know who to look for. He was at the war when Mom was born, and he doesn't even have a clue about me. *(He takes the photo from the box.)* Do you think he'd come back if he knew about me, Grandma?

GRANDMA. I know he would.

EVEN. Why did he go to the war?

GRANDMA. It was the law, inescapable as weather.

EVEN. Did he want to go?

GRANDMA. At first. He didn't really understand what was going on there. None of us did.

EVEN. Do you think he—

GRANDMA. No more war stories.

EVEN. Do you still miss him?

GRANDMA. Everyday, for years.

EVEN. Me too. Even if I never knew him.

GRANDMA. We'll leave our new address, in case he shows up. Okay you, foot check.

(EVEN takes off his shoes and socks and wiggles his feet.)

Let's see what you've been up to all day. I see you've been eating chocolate.

EVEN. How do you *do* that?

GRANDMA. One day I'll show you. Now into bed.

(He crawls into the sleeping bag. She tucks the dog in with him.)

Don't forget to pack Heinz in the morning.

EVEN. I'm going to let him ride up front with us, so he doesn't try to run away. He doesn't want to move, either. *(She does a little gesture, a good-night ritual.)* Grandma? You know that old box...

GRANDMA. It's staying, E.

EVEN. I know... but, I was wondering if you had a key for it.

GRANDMA. I lost it. A long time ago.

EVEN. Do you know what's inside?

GRANDMA. *No.* Goodnight. *(She begins to exit but EVEN still wants to talk.)*

EVEN. Grandma?

GRANDMA. You're talking in your sleep.

EVEN. Do you hate my dad?

GRANDMA. This is not a bedtime story, E. This is another war story.

EVEN. But do you?

GRANDMA. I don't hate him.

EVEN. You're mean to him.

GRANDMA. I never understood why your mother married that man. His family—his people—they were the one's your grandpa Olive fought against. Maybe I took it personally. I didn't understand how she could betray her own father that way.

EVEN. But I thought the war was over when they met.

GRANDMA. You don't remember war at arm's length, E. No matter how time passes. It preys on your mind, gets in your skin and your bones. It's a pain in your chest every night. If that makes me mean, so help me. *(Pause.)* Remembering brings nothing but sorrow. I want to put all those things that happened over there behind me. Put them in that old wooden box downstairs and leave them in this house. It's time to move on.

EVEN. But what if—

GRANDMA. Give the war a rest, Even. Sleep.

(She repeats the good-night gesture. He returns it.)

BLACKOUT

BORDER
by Silvia Gonzalez S.

CHARACTERS

NACHO: A used-car salesman-type.

ESTEFAN: A young man who normally goes about his own business. Not easily persuaded to do anything.

TIME: The present.
PLACE: A barren landscape.
There is a high fence blocking the view beyond.

AT RISE: *NACHO is digging under the fence. ESTAFAN enters and walks by, not noticing NACHO.*

NACHO. One dollar.
ESTAFAN *(startled, then suspicious)*. For what?
NACHO. To get to the other side.
ESTAFAN *(not completely in the dark with what is on the other side)*. What's on the other side?
NACHO. Gold.
ESTAFAN. What's on this side?
NACHO. Silver.
ESTAFAN. I like silver.
NACHO. One dollar.
ESTAFAN *(losing patience, wanting to leave)*. For what?
NACHO. To get to the other side. Do you want money?

51

ESTAFAN. Everyone wants money.

NACHO. Give me a dollar, and you can go to the other side through here, and see what you'll get.

ESTAFAN. What will I get?

NACHO. Whatever you want. You want money, you can get that, too. See that hole?

ESTAFAN. Yes.

NACHO. I dug it so you can go to the other side.

ESTAFAN. What's on the other side?

NACHO. I told you! More money.

ESTAFAN. Then why don't you go there?

NACHO. I've been there.

ESTAFAN. Then?

NACHO. I'm here to help others like you.

ESTAFAN. To get to the other side?

NACHO. That's right. One dollar.

ESTAFAN. Why do I want to go to the other side?

NACHO. For the money.

ESTAFAN. I don't care about the money.

NACHO. Everyone cares about money. Are you crazy? Money is the first step to get what you want. You want love? Then you need money to dress yourself nicely to get the attention from that special person. You want to be entertained, you need money to pay for the movie. You need money to go to Disneyland! Everything is expensive. It's not free!

ESTAFAN. What if I want to walk in the forest? Just to see trees, and wildflowers.

NACHO. That costs money, too. You have to buy gas to get there. You have a car? *(Pause. Knows the answer.)* You need money to buy one.

ESTAFAN *(slightly curious)*. The money is on the other side?

NACHO. I told you that. Weren't you listening?

ESTAFAN. Where exactly?

NACHO. You have to work for it.

ESTAFAN. I thought so. I knew there was a catch.

NACHO. Well, how else will you get it? That's the only way.

ESTAFAN. I can work here and make money.

NACHO. And you can work there, but for more money. You get much more for the work over there. NOW, just go through this hole and to the other side AND—

ESTAFAN *(interrupts)*. I already have a job. And I like it.

NACHO. How much does it pay?

ESTAFAN. Enough.

NACHO. On the other side, it pays even more than enough. And the extra, buy yourself a nice outfit, and see a funny movie with your date. Give me the dollar and I'll let you crawl through this hole. I made it with my bare hands. It's the perfect size for you.

ESTAFAN. I'll get dirty if I go through there.

NACHO. For another dollar, I'll put this plastic bag down so you won't get dirty.

ESTAFAN. No. *(He starts to walk away.)*

NACHO *(defeated)*. That's all right. I understand.

ESTAFAN *(stops to look back at NACHO)*. I'm sorry. I'm not interested.

NACHO. It doesn't matter to me. I'm just trying to help. That's all I try to do. So many like yourself hunger, and I try to assist. That's all. Make a little money, but mostly it is for people as unfortunate as you. You know yourself. It's all right. Go on your way.

ESTAFAN. You are making me feel bad. What did I do?

NACHO *(sincere)*. *Nothing*. That's the problem.

ESTAFAN. What do you mean?

NACHO. I'm just an honest man trying to make a living. Thank you very much for your time. *(Pause.)* Do you know anyone who would want to get to the other side? If you do, let them know I'm here. God bless you.

ESTAFAN *(trying to act slightly interested)*. What else is over there?

NACHO. Freedom.

ESTAFAN. Everyone has freedom.

NACHO. There's no freedom here.

ESTAFAN. I'm free to walk anywhere I like.

NACHO. There's no freedom if you can't make a lot of money.

ESTAFAN. You're making a dollar a person with that hole.

NACHO. As soon as *they* find out I'm doing it, I'll be kicked out. The horror is that someone else will take my place. And I've lost everything. That's the way it is here.

ESTAFAN. It is?

NACHO. Yes. Don't you know that already? Where have you been? Don't you see what is around you? Or are you content with what you have?

ESTAFAN. I don't know. I'm not sure now.

NACHO. The only way you'll know is by giving me a dollar, and going to the other side. You'll see what is waiting for you. You'll see wonderful things. Things you will want. Things that you'll get with extra hard work.

ESTAFAN. All you get is a dollar?

NACHO. Well, I get more. I get the satisfaction of helping someone into the world of fortune.

ESTAFAN *(suspicious)*. That's all?

NACHO. Well, I do get a bonus for directing you to certain places for jobs. And I'm glad you asked. In my pocket I have places to find work. It's guaranteed. All you have to do is take it to them—they'll know it came from me—and you get the job. Otherwise, you find your own.

ESTAFAN. How much?

NACHO. You've become smart already. Just by standing here with me. One dollar each. Three for three dollars.

ESTAFAN. I'll take three.

NACHO. Then you'll use the hole?

ESTAFAN. You have leads on jobs?

NACHO. Exactly. I thought I told you that before.

ESTAFAN. You didn't.

NACHO. My mistake. No wonder.

ESTAFAN. No wonder what?

NACHO. No wonder you weren't eager at the beginning about going to the other side.

ESTAFAN. I *wasn't* eager.

NACHO. What changed your mind?

ESTAFAN. I don't know exactly.

NACHO. You won't regret it. That'll be five dollars.

ESTAFAN. Five dollars!? Four!

NACHO. It's five!

ESTAFAN. For what?

NACHO. For the plastic.

ESTAFAN. I don't want the plastic.

NACHO. All right. Give me the money.

ESTAFAN. Here's a ten.

NACHO. Oh, I'm so sorry. All I have is a five. I can give you change later, eh?

ESTAFAN *(frustrated, and suspicious of his lack of change)*. Then just give me the plastic.

NACHO. Whatever you say.

(They exchange the money. NACHO digs the hole a little bigger for ESTAFAN. He lays the plastic around the hole. ESTAFAN then crawls underneath the wall. After a few moments, gunfire is heard. NACHO is surprised and worried; then the gunshots stop. He's full of false horror. He looks through the hole, then sticks his hand underneath. After some struggle, he pulls out the other five dollars. He brushes the dirt off the money and his pants. He sits on the ground to rest. In a few moments he sees someone coming in the distance and quickly goes into his salesman stance.)

NACHO. One dollar!

BLACKOUT

THE BAG OF CHIPS
by *Michael Schneider*

CHARACTERS

TWO TEENAGERS

TIME: The present.
PLACE: A classroom.

AT RISE: *A enters the classroom, sees B.*

A. Whoa!! We got a test today?

B. Yeah.

A. On, um, the...

B. *The Gift of the Magi.*

A. Right. Did you finish it?
   (B rolls eyes in contempt.)
   How does it end?
   (A, still standing, starts rummaging through bookbag.)

B. They get a divorce.

A. You're lying.

B. Read it yourself.

A. Dang. Can I borrow a pencil?

B. I don't think so. *(Pause; A is stunned.)* I'm not kidding.
   (A is staring pointedly at an extra sharpened pencil on B's desk; B holds it up, points to A's open bookbag.)
   Gimme your potato chips.
   (A starts to open a small bag of chips.)

B. No. The whole bag.

A. No way. *(A can see the contents of B's bookbag.)* You got two bags already. You got a whole lunch.

B. Un-hunh—

A. You don't need my chips. I have to have a pencil.

B. I'm glad you can see the situation so clearly.

A. It's not fair.

B. But it's the way things are. Those with the greatest need have to make the greatest sacrifices.

A. You're a jerk.

(A hands B the bag of chips. B hands over the pencil, places the bag of chips at the left front of his desktop, sits back and smiles smugly. Pause.)

They really get a divorce?

B. Can't remember. Maybe they live happily ever after.

A. Which?

B. Pick one.

(A leans over and smashes the bag of chips with the pencil.)

BLACKOUT

PASSIVE AGGRESSION
by Michael Schneider

CHARACTERS

TWO TEENAGERS: Siblings.

TIME: The present.
PLACE: School hallway and living room.

A *(dials pay phone in school hallway).*
B *(answering at home on couch).* Hello.
A. Is Mom home?
B. Well, don't say hello. Where are you?
A. I'm at school. Jason's mom never showed up.
B *(mock sympathy).* Awww.
A. Lemme talk to Mom.
B. Say please.
A *(silence).*
B. Oooh. I just heard the garage door. I think Mom's going out.
A. I'm in a bad mood. Don't play around.
B. No, it's true. In fact, I just heard the engine start.
A. Stop her!
B. I haven't got my shoes on. I'd freeze my little tooties.
A *(silence).*
B. This must be very frustrating for you. You're cold, hungry, you're gonna miss *(name of TV program).* Dinner was terrific. Not much left, though. Just the mashed po-

tatoes, and they're kinda cold and hard, you know how they get.

A *(pause)*. I'll just go see what I can find in your locker. *(Hangs up.)*

B. You stay out of my locker! *(Name)*, are you there?

MAKE YOUR OWN ENDING
BLACKOUT

CHARLIE IN LOVE
by Michael Schneider

CHARACTERS

CHARLIE: Teenager.
SISTER: His older teenage sister.

TIME: The present.
PLACE: Living room.

Note: Slash (/) mark indicates where next speaker starts overlapping.

AT RISE: *CHARLIE is sitting on the couch in trance-like state. His eyes are lightly closed, his head is slightly inclined, his mouth is open halfway. He is imagining kissing someone, but we can't tell that from watching. His movements are subtle, like the twitches of a dreaming dog. His sister enters, unheard.*

SISTER. Hello?!? Earth to Charles.
CHARLIE *(recovering)*. Uh, hi, how was school?
SISTER. What were you doing?
CHARLIE. Nothing.
SISTER. Yeah. Right! You had this retarded look on your face, like someone going to the/ bathroom.
CHARLIE. Shut up and leave me alone!
SISTER. Whoa! Sorreee.

(She sets her bookbag down on the table, opens it, takes out a water bottle, takes a swig, picks up the phone. CHARLIE reclines on the couch pretending to read.)

CHARLIE. Do you know Jackie Winters?

SISTER *(starting to dial)*. Yeah, she's a pig. She sat next to me in first grade, always had snot running out of her nose.

CHARLIE. Well, she doesn't have any snot running out of her nose now.

SISTER. What? Oh no, yuck! Not her! She's too old for you, Charlie.

CHARLIE. No she's not.

SISTER. That's what you were doing when I walked in, isn't it? Imagining going at it with Jackie Winters?

CHARLIE. You shut up. If you tell anyone, I'll... *(Suddenly pointing at the phone.)* is there someone on there?

SISTER. No. *(Putting it to her ear.)* Heather?

CHARLIE. Did she/ hear?

SISTER. Did you hear anything? Say no. *(To CHARLIE.)* No. *(Back to phone.)* Hi... Nothing—

CHARLIE *(interrupts)*. If she/ heard.

SISTER. Just a minute *(Covers mouthpiece; to CHARLIE.)* Relax. Your secret's safe. I just wish you had better taste.

(They stare at each other, seeking trust.)

BLACKOUT

WE ALWAYS FIND YOU
by *Silvia Gonzalez S.*

CHARACTERS

ROBERTO: A Mexican-American border-patrol officer.
MANUEL: Age 50, a frequent border trespasser.

TIME: The present.
PLACE: A lonely stretch of border between Mexico and
the United States.

AT RISE: *ROBERTO has just caught MANUEL sneaking
away from the border patrol's roundup at the border.*

MANUEL. Roberto! *Que me lleva la trampa.* Look, if you
catch me again, they'll think we are dating. Only lovers
meet together like this.
ROBERTO *(enjoying MANUEL's friendly personality).*
Manuel.
MANUEL *(eagerly).* ¿Si?
ROBERTO. Aye, Manuel. How many times do we have to
go through this?
MANUEL *(smiling).* I don't know. How many times?
One, two, three, four, five?
ROBERTO. We always find you.
MANUEL. Someday you won't find me. I'll already be
gone.
ROBERTO. This is the twentieth time.

MANUEL. Twenty? *(Thinks.)* No, much less.

ROBERTO. No, it's about twenty times.

MANUEL. Well, then, maybe you're right. But the last time you didn't shoot your gun. Are we losing respect for one another?

ROBERTO. No. I have lots of respect for you.

MANUEL. That's when I know you're like us. When you respect people much older than yourself. Thank you for stopping to say hello. *(He starts to exit.)*

ROBERTO. Don't you think you're getting too old for this behavior?

MANUEL. What? Looking for work? Aye, Roberto, what education you unfortunately lack! *(Patiently.)* *Mira,* when a man stops looking for work, it's time for him to die. If you don't work, then you don't deserve life. We learn that over there. Bad schools here, huh?

ROBERTO. They pay you shit.

MANUEL. Easy for you to say. They pay me more shit over there. I even smell it.

ROBERTO. It's illegal for you to come.

MANUEL. I know. Strange thing.

ROBERTO. Go towards the jeep like everyone else.

MANUEL. There's nothing over there for me. Just a couple of dollars from the tourists. Even *they* are getting stingy.

ROBERTO. You work your butt off.

MANUEL. Work is good.

ROBERTO. For low wages.

MANUEL. Work is good.

ROBERTO. In the jeep.

MANUEL *(comically).* You're the boss.

ROBERTO. I'm sending you home.

MANUEL. I am home, Roberto. Someone made a mistake with the history books. This all used to belong to Spain, then Mexico after the rebellion.

ROBERTO. It belonged to the Indians first.

MANUEL. Yes, but they liked us better than the English... Whatever you say, Mr. Part-Americano. It's probably in better hands now. Let me see your hands. Ehg, they're ugly. Go wash them. Let's go. Take me to the jeep, *jefe.*

ROBERTO. I'm doing my job.

MANUEL. And you're doing it so well. *(Silence. MANUEL puts out his hands for the handcuffs.)*

ROBERTO. Don't be stupid.

MANUEL. Roberto. Is it stupid to improve your life? Go ahead. You caught me.

ROBERTO. It's my job to return those who were born over there—

MANUEL *(overlapping on "over")*. Your grandfather was born over there. *(Pause.)* Aye, my friend. Do your job. I have a job, too. It's to survive in any way I can. Even to come where I'm not wanted. It's the last possible thing, believe me. I wouldn't do it if it was any better for me. Why humiliate myself? *(Long pause.)* Well, I go to the chariot that awaits me over there. The one that looks like a bus. Oh, you brought the van this time! Nice seat covers. How many of my compadres are you sending home? Hopefully some of them worked at least a day to cover expenses. *(Uncomfortable, yet a kind silence.)* Adios, señor gato. *(Starts to exit in the opposite direction from where the van is located.)*

ROBERTO. Manuel, the van is over there.

(MANUEL notices some weakness from ROBERTO for the first time and continues walking away from the van.)

ROBERTO. Manuel. Manuel!

(ROBERTO pulls out his gun.)

Freeze, Manuel. FREEZE.

(But ROBERTO just can't shoot. MANUEL escapes. Sounds of vehicles driving away.)

BLACKOUT

WHO WANTSTA KNOW
by *John O'Brien*

CHARACTERS

BOY: A teenager.
GIRL: A teenager.

TIME: The present.
PLACE: Sidewalk.

AT RISE: *BOY meets GIRL outside of school.*

BOY. You goin' home?
GIRL. Who wantsta know?
BOY. I do.
GIRL. Maybe I am.
BOY. May I carry your books?
GIRL. I ain't got no books.
BOY. Whatcha got in there?
GIRL. Who wantsta know?
BOY. I do.
GIRL. If you guess it, you can carry it.
BOY. A radio.
GIRL. It's all yours.
BOY. Whattaya listen to?
GIRL. Music.
BOY. What kinda music?
GIRL. The kind that makes me wanta move.

67

BOY. Me too.

GIRL. You like to move?

BOY. It runs in the family.

GIRL. Say what?

BOY. My old man's a mover.

GIRL. What does he move, pianos?

BOY. Himself. Whenever he fights with my mother, he moves out.

GIRL. It's a free country.

BOY. For some people.

GIRL. Don't take this personal, but why do you walk so slow?

BOY. I'm tryin' to make it last.

GIRL. Don't try too hard. Everything's gotta end.

BOY. I know.

GIRL. I hope you don't mind my askin', but have you got any friends?

BOY. Sure, I got friends.

GIRL. Who?

BOY. You.

GIRL. When did I say I was your friend?

BOY. It's not something you have to say.

GIRL. Why are you stopping?

BOY. This is your house.

GIRL. How do you know?

BOY. Just guessin'.

GIRL. I'm guessin' you've been here before.

BOY. I admit to having walked past here.

GIRL. How come?

BOY. Just walkin'.

GIRL. Don't jive with me. Howdya know where I live?

BOY. Since you put it that way ...

GIRL. I do.

BOY. I followed you.

GIRL. When?

BOY. Lotsa times.

GIRL. I never seen you followin' me.

BOY. Do you walk backwards?

GIRL. Only when the wind's blowin'.

BOY. That's why you never seen me.

GIRL. How come you followed me?

BOY. I was tryin' to build up my courage to talk to you.

GIRL. I'm glad you did.

BOY. Me too.

GIRL. Kin I have my radio back?

BOY. Sure.

GIRL. Thanks.

BOY. Kin I walk you home tomorrow?

GIRL. What if the wind's blowin'?

BOY. If it is, we'll both walk backwards. Okay?

GIRL. Okay.

BOY. Thanks. *(He starts to walk away.)*

GIRL. Hey.

BOY. What?

GIRL. Where ya goin'?

BOY. Home.

GIRL. You don't live that way. You live that way.

BOY. You're right. I do. *(He starts to walk away and stops.)* Hey.

GIRL. What'?

BOY. Howdya know where I live?

GIRL. Who wantsta know?

BLACKOUT

A THOUSAND SOLDIERS
by *Allison Gregory*

CHARACTERS

EVEN STEVEN NGUYEN: An Asian-American boy, 10.
JOEY OLIVE: A boy of 10.

TIME: The present.
PLACE: Even's bedroom.

A strange visitor, JOEY OLIVE, shows up very late on the night before EVEN STEVEN NGUYEN moves away from the house his grandfather grew up in—a grandfather whose whereabouts are unknown since he disappeared during the Vietnam War before EVEN knew him.

AT RISE: *EVEN crawls out of his sleeping bag, then drags a mysterious wooden box that his grandfather built out from behind a stack of cardboard boxes. He tries to open it, but it is securely locked; he gives up, then pushes the box over to the window and stands atop it, looking out. He tilts his head sideways, sticks a leg out, and raises his arms to steady himself as he tips further to the side. JOEY enters carrying a small bag.*

JOEY. Are you trying out for the circus?
EVEN *(loses his balance and falls)*. Whoa! Who are you? What do you think you're doing in my room?!

70

JOEY. My name is Joseph, but you can call me Joey. And this is *my* room.

EVEN. This is *my* room!

JOEY. Are you the kid who lives here now?

EVEN. That's right. 623 Oakdale Drive.

JOEY. I'm the kid who's moving in. I want to see where all my stuff is going to go.

EVEN. You can't just come in here and—

JOEY. It's kind of small.

EVEN. *Small?* Look at this! *(He opens up his empty closets.)* There's all sorts of neat space in here. My grandfather built all these shelves.

JOEY. Is he a carpenter?

EVEN. That's right.

JOEY. Do you think he could teach me to be one?

EVEN. He could if he were here.

JOEY. Where is he?

EVEN. I don't know.

JOEY. I can store all my records in there.

EVEN. Records are *totally historic.* No one except my grandma plays records anymore! Look, this is my room and no one is allowed in here except my best friends.

JOEY. It's only yours until midnight. My family takes possession at twelve-o-one.

EVEN. You better get out of here—

JOEY. Make me.

EVEN. I'll fight you!

JOEY. Oh yeah? *(They circle each other; then JOEY stops.)* You can have your stupid room.

EVEN. It's not a stupid room.

JOEY. I like my old room better. Plus I don't know how to fight.

EVEN. You don't know how to *fight*? Want me to teach you?

JOEY. No thanks. *(Pause.)* Okay.

EVEN. Come at me.

JOEY. What do you mean?

(EVEN puts his fists up in a sparring position. JOEY accepts the challenge. EVEN jabs at him.)

EVEN. Come on, block me, block me.

(JOEY tries, darting about, blocking EVEN as though swatting at flies. The sparring is quickly reduced to a laughing slap-fight between the two boys.)

JOEY *(breathless)*. How was that?

EVEN. We're going to have to work on your strategy.

(They lean against the boxes. JOEY looks at the photo.)

JOEY. Is this your dad? He doesn't even look like you.

EVEN. That's my grandfather at the war.

JOEY. Is he flying a kite?

EVEN. He sure is.

JOEY. The war must be fun!

EVEN. What have you got in that bag?

JOEY. Marbles.

EVEN. I collect rocks.

JOEY. What kind?

EVEN. All kinds. Well, just one.

JOEY. Can I see it?

EVEN. Can I see your marbles? *(Pause.)*

JOEY. Sure.

(EVEN sets the quartz out. JOEY dumps the marbles.)

EVEN. Those *rock*.

JOEY. Actually they're glass. *(He lifts one of them.)* This is my favorite: cat's-eye. It's a shooter. You can rub it for good luck.

EVEN. Niiice. This is my best one. (*He holds out the quartz.*)

JOEY. Want to trade?

EVEN. Are you crazy? One of my best friends gave this to me. (*Pause.*) Okay. (*They trade.*)

JOEY. How come you're moving away?

EVEN. My mom says the schools are better there.

JOEY. That's what my mom said.

EVEN. I guess other schools are always better than the one you're at.

JOEY. I don't want to go to a new school.

EVEN. You have to make all new friends.

JOEY. The teachers mess your name up.

EVEN. You don't get picked for teams just because you're *new.*

JOEY. I don't get picked for teams and I've been going there since first grade. Maybe we could run away.

EVEN. I would be grounded for the rest of my life.

JOEY. Me too. What's your name?

EVEN. Even Steven Nguyen.

JOEY. Even? Why did they name you that?

EVEN. I've got both sides in me. (*He steps onto the box at the window and tilts sideways.*)

JOEY. Why do you do that?

EVEN. I'm changing my perspective. It's a different way of seeing.

(*JOEY joins him. A faint but steady beat rises in the distance.*)

JOEY. Wow, look... (*The beat intensifies, thundering as it passes. It is the sound of marching.*)

EVEN. Soldiers? What are they doing here?

JOEY. Don't ask me, it's *your* neighborhood.

EVEN. There are hundreds of them.

JOEY. *Thousands.*

(EVEN goes to the window and tosses the rope out.)
What are you going to do with that rope?

EVEN. Escape.

JOEY. Are you running away?

EVEN. Just for tonight. Those soldiers might know where my grandfather is. I have to find out about him.

JOEY. What about your mom?

EVEN. She doesn't have to know, she'll only worry. We just have to make sure to be back by morning.

JOEY. *We?*

EVEN. You said you wanted him to teach you to be a carpenter.

JOEY. Yeah, but...

EVEN. Bring his picture, Joey.

JOEY. Why do you want his picture?

EVEN. So we know him if we see him. Do you want to help me find him or not?

JOEY. Do you want to be best friends? *(Pause.)*

EVEN. Okay.

JOEY. You go first. *(Picks up the photo.)* I hope nobody asks what we're doing, because I can't lie. I *blink.*

EVEN. You won't have to lie, Joey. We'll be back before anyone knows. *(He grabs the rope and jumps up onto the windowsill.)*

JOEY. Hey, Even? When I learn how, I'm going to build you a real ladder.

EVEN. That's great, Joey. *(Drops out of sight.)*

JOEY. Jeepers creepers.

BLACKOUT

BEST FRIENDS DON'T BITE
by Joanna H. Kraus

CHARACTERS

CHRISTABEL: Fourteen-year-old paraplegic, as a result of a recent accident. Angry, attractive high school freshman. In a wheelchair.

VICTOR: Sixteen-year-old high-school junior. Volunteer at the Redwood Medical Center. Mature, amiable, good-looking.

TIME: An autumn Sunday afternoon. The present.
PLACE: A parking lot and the front seat of an old car.

Note: Dialogue in italics represents the thoughts of the characters. Although the lines are spoken aloud, so the audience can hear them, VICTOR doesn't hear CHRIS-TABEL's thoughts, nor does she hear his.

AT RISE: *A furious CHRISTABEL in her wheelchair, heads for the car, which is represented by a bench with steering wheel attached. VICTOR walks beside her. Both are dressed up.*

VICTOR. Wow! That trumpet player was fantastic! *(She doesn't respond.)* You're awfully quiet, Christabel. Are you tired? First time out on the town.

CHRISTABEL. You sound like my mother! I'm not an invalid!

VICTOR. Hey, I know that! Just want to make sure you're OK. Boy, I could have listened to that narrator all afternoon. Do you think she'll be famous? *(Smiles agreeably.)* Then you and I can say we saw her when!

CHRISTABEL. You had to tell her I had an accident, didn't you? Like she cared that I fell off a twenty-foot ladder! In case you haven't noticed, Victor, there are no Sunday receptions for a T-5!

VICTOR. Are you mad at me? *(She doesn't answer.)*

Some first date this is turning out to be!

Christabel, I bent rules to take you to the concert today. Even had to get permission!

CHRISTABEL. *Chill! You don't have to give him the deep freeze.*

(They have reached the car. VICTOR mimes opening the door. CHRISTABEL transfers from her wheelchair to the bench. VICTOR sneaks admiring looks at her as she easily transfers into the car, but when she glances at him he quickly looks the other way. VICTOR folds the chair up and stores it in the trunk.)

CHRISTABEL *(as she glides from chair to bench).*

Terrific! See, those hours of practice paid off.

(Melts slightly.)

Nice, the casual way he puts Gerry in the trunk—like he did it every day. And he was right about naming it. Better than saying "the chair" for the next seventy-five years!

(Sound: motor starting. Behind the wheel, VICTOR moves out of the parking lot onto the highway. He is whistling some of the classical music they just heard.)

VICTOR. Are you upset because I stopped to talk to the narrator?

CHRISTABEL. Getting warmer.

VICTOR. She made me think of my sister, Elena.

CHRISTABEL. Sure.

VICTOR. Christabel, I'm too old to play Twenty Questions. I never liked that game anyway.

CHRISTABEL *(forgets herself)*. Me neither!

VICTOR. So up until an hour ago, we were friends. What happened?

CHRISTABEL. You want me to be honest?

VICTOR. We always have been. That's one of the things I admire about you.

And you're bright and pretty and your laugh is like wind chimes.

CHRISTABEL. Did you know?

VICTOR *(affable)*. That's not an answer. That's a question! You're the straight-A English student.

CHRISTABEL. Victor, did you know?

VICTOR. Know what?

CHRISTABEL. Was that your idea of a Sunday school lesson?

VICTOR. Christabel, what are you talking about?

CHRISTABEL *(angry)*. You know. Blind lady inspires the crip! *(VICTOR jams on the brakes. Sound: brakes squealing. He parks the car.)*

Why are we stopping? I have to get home.

VICTOR *(furious)*. Not till we straighten this out. Do you know how long I've waited for this afternoon? Wanting to take you to something we'd both enjoy? Classical trumpet for me. Theatre for you. So when I saw the poster for Stravinsky's *The Soldier's Tale*, I thought, that's perfect! Finally I persuaded Bud to let me take you. But my boss and your physical therapist warned me nothing too long. Nothing too stressful. So I listened to the record first. Timed it. One hour, five minutes. Then I checked if the hall was really wheelchair-accessible, because sometimes they say it is, but no one's ever tried it out, or there's a couple of stairs. Then I called to ask if we could sit together in a place we could both see and hear well, and I even went back to check, because I didn't want us behind a post or so far away we'd need binoculars. I didn't just buy the tickets, Christabel, I organized a field trip! *(A strained voice.)* I wanted this afternoon to be special—for both of us. I've never seen you outside the hospital.

CHRISTABEL. Victor, I—

VICTOR. I got a haircut for you. I washed the car for you. And waxed it. And you didn't even notice!

CHRISTABEL. It's just that—

VICTOR. Let me finish! Do you know why I did all that? Do you? *(A confession.)* For the first time I wanted to share music that's important to me with someone who's important to me!

CHRISTABEL. *Did you hear him? He said "important"! Thaw out. Who's spent every Friday afternoon for the last two months in the Redwood Medical Center cafeteria helping you with algebra? Best friends don't bite!*

VICTOR. So the narrator was blind. Big deal! She sees with her ears. She sees with her soul. There's different ways to see. Elena taught me that. And there's different ways to walk. You were walking to the music. No, you were dancing, swaying just slightly. Smiling. I saw you.

You were beautiful, Christabel. You made me feel glad we were there together, sitting so close. I wanted to hug you right then and there! But Friday afternoon Bud took me aside and reminded me no romantic stuff while you're a patient. See, you're his patient and even though I'm just his nonpaid volunteer, technically I'm staff. He figured out why I changed my volunteer time.

CHRISTABEL. Victor, you still didn't answer my question.

VICTOR. To answer your question, no! I didn't know. Heck, no one could tell until the soldier guided her offstage! That's why I wanted to meet her. For Elena. No, I didn't know she was blind. Does that make her acting any more—or less? I feel sorry for you, Christabel. *(She shivers.)* Oh, not because you're in a chair! But because you have such tunnel vision, that it's all you can think about! Fifty-four million other Americans have disabilities, and they get on with their lives. Damn it, Christabel, didn't anyone ever teach you to say thank you?

(They stare moodily out the window.)

WHOA! *Too far!*

CHRISTABEL. *Are you trying to chase him away or what? I thought you broke your spine, not your head!*

VICTOR. *I should have just kept it at the center. Bud said there are reasons why they don't want staff getting involved with patients, especially when they're ... vulnerable.*

(Looks over at her.)

Vulnerable! More like a tiger!

CHRISTABEL. *I ruined it. My first date.*

(Miserably.)

And probably my last! If it weren't for Elena, how would he know how I feel? He's been there. Remember going back to school? He knew how scared I was. He made me listen to "The Triumphal March" and told me to hear it in my head when I opened the classroom door. And it worked! So, apologize.

VICTOR. *Sometimes I want to shake her! Doesn't she know how smart she is? Except for algebra. That was a lucky break for me! And when we talk, half the time we could finish each other's sentences. We're like part of a puzzle that goes together. So, apologize. Hey, she started the fight!*

CHRISTABEL. *This silence is awful! Wonder if outer space is like that. Maybe some of what he said is ... sort of true. But he didn't have to be so rude. How'd he like a life sentence at age fourteen and a half.*

(Sneaks a look at him.)

His hands are golden tan. Sort of square-shaped. I wish I dared touch just a finger ...

(Looks down at her shoes, her hands clenched in her lap.)

VICTOR. *Funny how silence vibrates. Like music that's there all the time; but you can't hear it until you listen. Really listen. What'll it cost to say, "I'm sorry"?*

CHRISTABEL. *Say "Boo," say, "Hello," say, "Take me home," try, "I'm sorry."*

(Awkwardly they turn toward each other.)

CHRISTABEL & VICTOR *(simultaneously).* I'm sorry.
VICTOR. I ran off at the mouth. *(He traces a finger around her face, as if he's memorizing it.)*

CHRISTABEL *(gently).* You're thinking about Elena, aren't you?

VICTOR. Whenever I leave L.A., she does that. "My fingers are my camera," she says. Funny thing about divorce. It shouldn't separate brother and sister, but it does.

CHRISTABEL. Would she have liked the concert?

VICTOR. You bet! *(Pause.)* And you. She'd like you.

CHRISTABEL. Even...just now?

VICTOR. Even...just now. *(Smoothing the frown on her forehead.)* She'd understand. You'll meet her someday.

CHRISTABEL *(in a rush).* This afternoon was the best time I've had since before—

VICTOR. The accident?

CHRISTABEL *(nods; serious).* Victor, it's a little late, but thank you.

VICTOR *(grins).* It's a little late, but you're welcome.

CHRISTABEL. Are we...are we still friends?

VICTOR *(squeezes her hand tightly).* Till the finish line.

CHRISTABEL. *Wish I could stand up for five seconds. Close to him. Maybe... Whoa! Reality check. Did you ever see an ad, "Handsome guy wants crippled girl?" He's a friend!*

(She looks around the car, tries to make amends.) You cleaned it so well, it looks brand new. Sort of sparkles.

VICTOR. Took me hours. Ten years old. I was six when this car was built, and now it's my buddy. *(Joking.)* The only part of my life that never gives me trouble.

CHRISTABEL *(settling in)*. It's cozy. *(He smiles over at her.)* You could almost live in it!

VICTOR. Sometimes I wish I could.

CHRISTABEL. Funny how when parents divorce you have two homes but no home.

VICTOR. Yeah. *(Looks at her, then looks at dashboard.)* Guess I better get you home.

CHRISTABEL *(sighs contentedly and whispers)*. I am home. *(Embarrassed, she covers her mouth.)*

VICTOR *(eyes shining, leans over and kisses her on the cheek)*. Christabel. *(He lingers, and she smiles up at him.)*

CHRISTABEL *(breathes in)*. Umm. You smell...spicy.

VICTOR *(lifts her hair gently and breathes in the fragrance)*. Your hair smells like lemon and lime.

And sunshine and springtime.

(Mumbles.) RMC's got these rules. About patients and staff. *(Puts keys in ignition.)* I'm staff.

(CHRISTABEL runs her fingers lightly around the spot he's just kissed.)

CHRISTABEL *(surprised)*. Watch out, clouds! Move over, stars! He likes me! HE LIKES ME!

(They steal glances at each other. Sound: motor starting. Their smiles could light a birthday cake. Sound: a few phrases of a joyous trumpet solo.)

BLACKOUT

THE GO-GO GIRL
by John O'Brien

CHARACTERS

GIRL ONE: A teenager.
GIRL TWO: A teenager.

TIME: The present.
PLACE: Anywhere.

AT RISE: *Two girls are strolling down the street.*

GIRL ONE. So I go: "I'll call ya tonight," and he goes: "If you're lucky," so I go: "Who do you think you are?" and he goes: "I'll show you who I am," and I go: "It's about time you did," and he goes: "What's that supposeda mean?" and I go: "Take it any way you want to," and he goes: "I'll take it or leave it," and I go: "What's that supposeda mean?" and he goes: "Guess," and he goes and hangs up, and I go and pull the phone plug outta the wall, and my mudda looks up from her soap operas for the first time in three days, and she goes: "Whatsa matter?" and I go: "That fink-head I go out wid just hung up on me," and she goes: "Don't sweat it. He'll call back. They all do," and I go: "He can't call back. I just broke the phone," and she goes: "If you broke it, fix it," and I go: "I can't fix it," and she goes: "Why not?" and I go: "'Cause I don't

84

know how," and she goes: "Find out how," and I go: "How am I supposeda find out how?" and she goes: "Go to school," and I go: "I do go to school," and she goes: "Pay attention to your teachas," and I go: "My teachas don't teach fixin' phones," and she goes: "Judgin' by you, they don't teach nuttin', and if you keep this up, young lady, I'll tell your father," and I go: "If you wait until he's sober, you'll hafta wait until the day after the day after Christmas," and she goes: "That's enough of that. Your father worked hard all his life to give you everything you have," and I go: "What've I got?" and she goes: "You've got a bed to sleep in, clothes on your back, food in your belly, and a color TV," and I go: "Everybody has that," and she goes: "That shows how much you know," and I go: "Do you know anybody that don't got a color TV?" and she goes: "There's lotsa people that don't," and I go: "But do you know anybody that don't?" and she goes: "Don't get smart wid me, young lady," and I go: "I'm supposeda get smart. That's why I go to school," and she goes: "I don't know what they teach you in that school, but when I went there, they taught us to respect our parents," and I go: "I musta been absent that day," and she goes: "I shoulda been absent the day you was born," and I go: "I thought you were," and she goes: "What's that supposeda mean?" and I go ...

GIRL TWO. Tell me tomorrow.

GIRL ONE. What's wrong with today?

GIRL TWO. I gotta go.

GIRL ONE. To the bathroom?

GIRL TWO. Not to the bathroom, to my house.

GIRL ONE. You don't got a bathroom in your house?

GIRL TWO. I got a bathroom in my house, but I'm not goin' to the bathroom. I'm goin' to my house.

GIRL ONE. You never go to your house. What're ya goin' to your house for?

GIRL TWO. If you must know ...

GIRL ONE. I must.

GIRL TWO. I'm expecting.

GIRL ONE. A baby?

GIRL TWO. A phone call.

GIRL ONE. You never get a phone call.

GIRL TWO. I'm gettin' one today.

GIRL ONE. Who from?

GIRL TWO. If you must know ...

GIRL ONE. I must.

GIRL TWO. My boyfriend.

GIRL ONE. You don't got a boyfriend.

GIRL TWO. I have one now.

GIRL ONE. Anybody I know?

GIRL TWO. Think about it. *(She exits.)*

GIRL ONE *(calling after her)*. What's that supposeda mean?

BLACKOUT

LESSONS FOR LIFE
by Jett Parsley

CHARACTERS

BESS: Age 18.
CLARINE: Her sister, age 14.

TIME: The present.
PLACE: A barn.

CLARINE is hoping to learn how the older kids act at parties so that she can seem cool at her first party tonight. BESS has had two boyfriends lately: Tib, whom CLARINE adores, and Billy, whom CLARINE despises.

AT RISE: *Lights up on BESS and CLARINE sitting on the barn floor. Both are dressed in jeans and T-shirts. BESS hands a cigarette to CLARINE.*

BESS. You always let the man light it.
(CLARINE puts the cigarette in her mouth and waits.)
And when he leans over, you have to sort of smile...
(CLARINE smiles awkwardly, eager to learn, but not quite getting it.)
That's all right. And you look sideways out of your eyes.
(CLARINE turns her head to the side and looks out of the corners of her eyes. BESS laughs.)

Shoot. Good thing Daddy don't keep animals in this barn. You'd scare 'em to death. Like this. You be the man.

(She gives CLARINE the lighter and puts a cigarette in her mouth. The cigarette lit, she takes a long, languorous puff.)

You see?

CLARINE. I was doin' that.

BESS. You weren't doin' that. If you need extras, I have some hidden in the feedbox.

CLARINE. Where do you hide the beer?

BESS. They drinkin' at this party tonight?

CLARINE. Could be.

BESS. Let's get the smokin' down first. You can't jump in it all at once. So...once it's lit, then you can talk 'bout him, mostly. Don't never talk about no one but the two of you.

CLARINE. My cigarette ain't lit.

(BESS lights it. CLARINE chokes, holds it in as well as she can. She gets her breath.)

What if he wants to talk about someone else?

BESS. Honey, if you're doin' it right, he won't.

CLARINE. What if he don't want to talk?

BESS. What do you think he's gonna want?

CLARINE. You're the teacher.

BESS. That ain't in today's lesson.

CLARINE. Oh, come on.

BESS. If he don't want to talk, blow smoke in his face and leave.

CLARINE. I can't do that!

BESS. Well, you can't do anything else.

CLARINE. Why not?

BESS. 'Cause it'll get you in trouble, that's why.

CLARINE. *You* do it.

BESS. I'm five years older. And even that don't mean I stay out of trouble.

CLARINE. How 'bout just kissin'. You can tell me about that, can't you?

BESS. Just kissin'?

CLARINE. You said once I was fourteen and Daddy let me go out with boys you'd show me these things. I been fourteen a week, and I still don't know—

BESS. Well, some things can't be taught.

CLARINE. I got my first party tonight—

BESS. Trust me. You got to leave some things to...practice.

CLARINE. I'm not sayin' I want to kiss *you*. I'll—I'll close my eyes and imagine. You just tell me what happens. I'll see it in my head.

BESS. *Just* kissin'.

(CLARINE nods.)

All right. So close your eyes.

(CLARINE closes her eyes.)

You're gonna bring him back here, right?

(CLARINE nods.)

Well, so you're here. He...he looks at you, I guess. Kinda funny, he looks.

CLARINE *(eyes still closed)*. Funny how?

BESS. I don't know. You...know...he wants to kiss you. He wants to put his hands on your waist, so you let him, and he pulls—

CLARINE *(opening her eyes)*. Wait a minute. You still ain't told me what it looks like.

BESS. Well, I don't know! I mean, I ain't never thought about it this way. It's a feelin' you get...somethin' gushes inside—

CLARINE. No good. What does *he* look like?

(BESS thinks.)

What did Tib look like when he wanted to?

BESS *(stamping out her cigarette, angry).* There you go bringin' up Tib again.

CLARINE. He's an example.

BESS. A bad one.

CLARINE. He don't kiss? What kind of stuff did he want to do?

BESS. Honey, it ain't what *they* want to do. It's what *you* want to do. That's why I can't tell you how a guy looks. 'Cause in that moment, you ain't thinkin' 'bout what he wants or how he looks. You're thinkin' 'bout you—you!

CLARINE. And what do *you* want? *(Scornfully.)* Billy Raikes?

BESS. Don't start on Billy now.

CLARINE. Billy'd put a dog collar 'round your neck and drag you down the street if you'd let him.

BESS. But I don't.

CLARINE. Tib don't make me feel like some worm weaslin' in.

BESS. Let me tell you somethin', Clarine. Tib may be nice. He may be sweet and treat girls right, but that don't mean every girl wants a guy like that. You, you got a nice streak in you and maybe someone like Tib's okay for you. But that ain't everyone's story.

(BILLY steps into the doorway. BESS looks toward him and speaks coyly.)

BESS. Sometimes a little honest meanness is what you need.
(CLARINE sees BILLY and stiffens.)
  Go on in the house, Clarine.
(CLARINE doesn't move.)
  You got chores don't you?
CLARINE *(in a hiss)*. Daddy don't like Billy Raikes, and you know it.
BESS. He ain't never said nothin'.
CLARINE. You said today you'd teach me to blow circles with the smoke.
BESS. You got plenty of time to learn that.
CLARINE. But what am I gonna do at the party if a—
BESS. It's all playactin', Clarine. Just remember that. Everyone's playactin'. Now run on. This is a private scene.

BLACKOUT

THE PRETENDER
by *John O'Brien*

CHARACTERS

BOY: Teenager.
GIRL: Teenager.

TIME: The present.
PLACE: School corridor.

AT RISE: *GIRL and BOY, walking from opposite direc-
tions, collide, dropping their books.*

BOY. Excuse me.
GIRL. Excuse me.
BOY. I'm sorry.
GIRL. Me too.
BOY. My fault.
GIRL. No, mine.

(They start picking up their books.)

BOY. I wasn't looking.
GIRL. Neither was I.
BOY. I was thinking.
GIRL. So was I.
BOY. About something else.
GIRL. Same here.

BOY. I've forgotten what it was.

GIRL. Mutual likewise.

BOY. I guess I can't think and look at the same time.

GIRL. I never could.

BOY. Don't tell anybody I asked you this, but which way was I going?

GIRL. West.

BOY. Which way is west?

GIRL. That way is east, so that way must be west.

BOY. How do you know that way is east?

GIRL. Because that's where the sun comes up.

BOY. The sun doesn't come up.

GIRL. Is that so?

BOY. We rotate around the sun.

GIRL. You don't say.

BOY. Every time the earth turns, we see the sun.

GIRL. Amazing.

BOY. The sun doesn't come up, and it doesn't go down.

GIRL. What does it do?

BOY. It doesn't do much of anything. It just turns round and round.

GIRL. Like us?

BOY. Something like us, but more on schedule.

GIRL. Does it ever get confused and forget which way it was going?

BOY. Never.

GIRL. Are you sure?

BOY. Absolutely.

GIRL. I'm impressed.

BOY. You don't sound impressed.

GIRL. I didn't mean I was impressed with your brilliance. I meant I was impressed with your arrogance.

BOY. Are you referring to my supercilious attitude, my *hauteur*, my overweening sense of hubris, my ineffably ineluctable intellectuality?

GIRL. I'll settle for snob.

BOY. Is knowledge snobbery?

GIRL. People who really know what they're talking about are never as sure as you are.

BOY. I'm only sure when I'm certain.

GIRL. Nothing is certain.

BOY. Are you sure?

GIRL. I'm only sure of one thing.

BOY. What's that?

GIRL. That I have better things to do with my time than to continue this conversation.

BOY. Like what?

GIRL. Like reading.

BOY. What are you reading?

GIRL. *Crime and Punishment*

BOY. Why read it? I'll tell you about it.

GIRL. I'd rather read it.

BOY. Why? Is Dostoyevsky more eloquent than I?

GIRL. He has one big advantage over you.

BOY. He's Russian?

GIRL. He's dead.

BOY. I'll be dead someday.

GIRL. When you are, I'll read your books.

BOY. What if YOU die first?

GIRL. If I die before you do, at least I won't have to read your books. I'll have to be content with Dostoyevsky.

BOY. Actually, I have moved beyond Dostoyevsky. I'm in my James Joyce period.

GIRL. Are you?

BOY. I may be the only high school student in the Western Hemisphere who has read *Finnegan's Wake*.

GIRL. What about the Eastern Hemisphere?

BOY. I didn't want to mention it. Among my friends, I'm famous for my modesty.

GIRL. You have friends?

BOY. I had one once.

GIRL. What happened?

BOY. She died.

GIRL. I'm sorry.

BOY. Hamsters don't live forever.

GIRL. Are you really a student here?

BOY. I just transferred.

GIRL. From outer space?

BOY. From seven different military bases.

GIRL. You're a secret weapon?

BOY. My father's a soldier.

GIRL. An officer, of course.

BOY. Of course.

GIRL. A general, no doubt.

BOY. I wasn't going to mention it.

GIRL. Did he teach you to march?

BOY. Before I could walk.

GIRL. Then YOU march west, and I'll march east.

BOY. Same time tomorrow?

GIRL. If you're lucky.

BOY. There's no such thing as luck.

GIRL. Since when?

BOY. There is only fate, destiny, what the Buddhists call karma.

GIRL. Am I your karma?

BOY. You are mine. I am yours. Same time tomorrow?

GIRL. Let me think.

BOY. Don't think. Follow your heart.

GIRL. Aye, aye, Captain.

BOY. That's navy. I'm army. Or my father is.

GIRL. Is that really true?

BOY. Is anything?

GIRL. Yes.

BOY. What?

GIRL. It's true that I'm going now. Goodbye.

BOY. Goodbye.

GIRL. Hey.

BOY. What?

GIRL. Where are my Cliff Notes on *Crime and Punishment*?

BOY. I have them. Here. Here they are.

GIRL. And what am I doing with the Cliff Notes on *Finnegan's Wake*?

BOY. They're mine. Don't get the wrong idea. I'm not reading them. I wrote them.

GIRL. And a letter from the state penitentiary. *(Long beat.)* I'm sorry.

BOY. That's all right.

GIRL. I didn't ask your name.

BOY. Cliff.

GIRL. Mine's Carmella. My friends call me Karma.

BOY. Is that true?

GIRL. Is anything?

BLACKOUT

SCENES WITH MULTIPLE
CHARACTERS

ANOTHER SATURDAY NIGHT
by *Sandra Fenichel Asher*

CHARACTERS

RADIO ANNOUNCER: Amplified offstage voice, any age, either gender.

MICHAEL PAEGLIS (PIE-yay-gleess): 17, restless.

BUDDY: His friend, 17, happy-go-lucky, may be male or female.

STATE TROOPER: Any age, either gender.

TIME: The present, early summer.
PLACE: The resort town of Braden's Port, N.J.

BEFORE RISE: *Rock music is heard playing loudly on Michael's car radio.*

AT RISE: *MICHAEL and BUDDY, lifelong friends who have just finished their junior year of high school, sit facing the audience in chairs representing the front seat of Michael's car. MICHAEL is driving, going nowhere in particular, looking glum. BUDDY is lip-synching or singing along to the music and bouncing to the beat. The song ends.*

RADIO ANNOUNCER. Star light! Star bright! It's Saturday night! And summer's in sight! As for you lucky people, you're tuned to WBPJ in Braden's Port, New Jersey. The coolest wave on the beach. A-rockin' and a-rollin' for you, twenty-four—I say, *twenty-four* hours a day. So what do we have here for our ultra-mellow listening public? Ninth caller? Ninth caller! We have dinner for you! Dinner for two! At the Jolly Mackerel, seafood so fresh you can almost hear the mermaids...

BUDDY *(turns the volume way down during the last of the above spiel and sighs happily)*. Another Saturday night in Braden's Port! What could be finer?

MICHAEL *(less than enthusiastic)*. What, indeed?

BUDDY *(looks suspiciously at MICHAEL)*. Something wrong with another Saturday night in Braden's Port? Coolest wave on the beach?

MICHAEL. No. *(Pause.)* Yes.

BUDDY. Maybe? All of the above? None of the above? Finals are over, Paeglis. Summer vacation is not a multiple-choice question.

MICHAEL. I know. It's just—it's just that when you've seen one Saturday night in Braden's Port, you've seen them all.

BUDDY. Meaning?

MICHAEL. Meaning, first we cruise around town or take in a movie. Then we go to Sweet Polly's for a hot fudge sundae. Then we cruise around town some more and stop at somebody's house to see what's up.

BUDDY *(all for it)*. Yeah! I wonder what's up?

MICHAEL. What's up is a bunch of guys sitting around talking about baseball and girls. Couple of girls show up and haul off a couple of guys. Somebody gets drunk and loud. Somebody else gets drunk and throws up. The rest of us send out for pizza.

BUDDY. Sounds good to me.

MICHAEL. Everything sounds good to you, Buddy.

BUDDY. Not everything—*this. This* sounds good. Well, maybe not the barf bags, but the rest of it. Since when is contentment a crime?

(MICHAEL hits the accelerator hard. BUDDY'S head is jolted back with the thrust.)

Hey, what's your hurry?

(MICHAEL ignores him, glares straight ahead.)

What're we doing on the highway?

(Still no answer.)

Michael! Where are you going?!

MICHAEL *(without letting up on the intensity of his driving).* Nowhere. Same as always.

BUDDY. What's eating you, Paeglis? It's June, man. Haven't you noticed?

MICHAEL. Look: We've been coming to Braden's Port with our folks every summer since we were kids, right?

BUDDY. Yup! Great life if you can get it, and we got it.

MICHAEL. But it never changes. *We* never change.

BUDDY. We didn't cruise when we were seven. We didn't even send out for our own pizza.

MICHAEL. Buddy, if you want me to explain what's bothering me, you're going to have to listen for more than five seconds at a time without cracking a joke.

BUDDY. Sorry. Force of habit. But my point remains: Things *have* changed, and they're still changing. For the better. We're going to be seniors in the fall, man. We're going to college. And then it's—

MICHAEL. *More of the same.* We major in business. We work with our families. We end up living their lives all over again. Winters in the suburbs, summers at the beach. How did we get locked in this way?

BUDDY *(amazed that this scenario bothers MICHAEL).* Don't you mean "How did we get so lucky?"

MICHAEL. I don't feel lucky. I feel like my life's closing in on me. Don't you ever wish you could—oh, I don't know—go out and—seek your fortune?

BUDDY. Slaughter dragons, you mean? Rescue damsels in distress? Is that what you're after?

MICHAEL. Well—something like that.

BUDDY. You read too much, Paeglis. Check out reality. You've got it so good, you don't know how good you've got it.

(MICHAEL shakes his head ruefully. BUDDY starts to turn up music, but then notices a siren in the distance. He listens as it grows louder. MICHAEL is lost in thought.)

Paegils? *(Turns off music.)* Michael? *(Realizes siren and now flashing red lights are for them.)* HEY! Earth to Michael Paeglis! The state troopers in your rear-view mirror are closer than they appear!

MICHAEL *(mimes putting on brakes and pulling off road).* Oh, man!

BUDDY. Nice work, pal.

(Siren fades. Red light continues flashing as TROOPER, tough and humorless, approaches MICHAEL's side of car.)

TROOPER. Name?

MICHAEL *(mumbling nervously).* Paeglis, sir.

TROOPER. What? What did you just say to me?

MICHAEL *(really nervous now, but louder).* Michael Paeglis, sir.

TROOPER. Oh. How old are you, Paeglis?

MICHAEL. Seventeen, sir. Eighteen in November, sir. November twenty-third, sir.

TROOPER. Let's see the driver's license.

(MICHAEL fumbles a wallet out of his pocket, opens it and hands it to TROOPER, who looks back and forth between MICHAEL and license several times, points to license.)

What's this say?

MICHAEL. Paeglis. Sir.

TROOPER. Unusual name.

MICHAEL. It's Latvian. Sir.

TROOPER. Latvian?

MICHAEL *(babbling).* One of three Baltic countries, sir: Estonia, Latvia, Lithuania. Formerly part of the Soviet Union. My father immigrated with his parents as a child. That is, my father was the child. His parents were—fully grown.

BUDDY *(stage whisper).* Michael—*enough.*

MICHAEL *(deflated; to TROOPER).* Sir.

TROOPER. Ever been in trouble before, Paeglis?

MICHAEL. No, sir, sir!

(BUDDY snorts; MICHAEL throws him an angry look. TROOPER looks in at BUDDY, who backs off.)

TROOPER *(nods thoughtfully; passes wallet back to MICHAEL).* Pay attention now, Michael. I'm going to let you off this time. Slow down, son. That's a warning. One warning to a customer. Got it?

MICHAEL. Yes...sir.

TROOPER. Be careful getting off this shoulder. Drive safely, son.

MICHAEL *(greatly relieved)*. I will, sir. Thank you, sir.

(TROOPER exits. Red light stops flashing. BUDDY watches TROOPER'S car as MICHAEL stares at his wallet.)

BUDDY. He's gone. *(To MICHAEL.)* Where did all those "sirs" come from?

MICHAEL. I don't know. The uniform brought back every war movie I've ever seen.

BUDDY. Man, that was close! Ah, well, not to worry. Your dad would've paid the ticket anyway. Remember the time you backed out of your driveway into a garbage truck—?

MICHAEL *(exasperated, snaps wallet shut angrily)*. That does it! I quit!

BUDDY. Quit what?

MICHAEL. My whole life! I can't stand it anymore! I'm a teenage boy who can't even get a speeding ticket! I'm so clean, I squeak! State troopers call me "son."

BUDDY. He wasn't planning to adopt you—

MICHAEL *(not amused)*. I'm going through life in a plastic bubble. Don't you see? Like that kid on TV who couldn't fight off disease. All he ever wanted was to walk barefoot in the grass, did you know that? And he never got the chance.

BUDDY. And all you ever wanted was a speeding ticket? Get back on the highway. Find that cop. I'm sure you could talk him into it.

MICHAEL. I don't know what I want, Buddy. I want to *find out* what I want. Out there—in the real world. I want to find out how it works.

BUDDY *(turning serious for the moment)*. Do you really?

MICHAEL. Yes!

BUDDY *(shaking his head sadly)*. Then you're a fool, Michael. A lot of it's out of order. That's why we have doors and windows that lock. Not to mention state troopers. Why take chances?

MICHAEL. You think you can hide behind those locked doors forever?

BUDDY. I sure intend to try.

MICHAEL. And are you sure I'm the fool here?

(BUDDY and MICHAEL exchange a look but do not reconcile. Disgusted, MICHAEL turns up the radio volume, then pulls car back onto highway. BUDDY looks concerned, mystified. Then BOTH stare ahead, facing the oncoming highway.)

RADIO ANNOUNCER. Are you out there, ninth caller? I know you're out there somewhere, so give it up and give us a call. Five-five-five seven-four-three-zero. You're listening to WBPJ in Braden's Port, New Jersey—the coolest wave on the beach. Oh, yes, we are afloat among the summertime stars, and we are inviting you to join us! Hear that, ninth caller? We are still waiting! What—I say, what have you got to lose?

(Music plays. MICHAEL and BUDDY cruise on into the night.)

BLACKOUT

HAIRCUT
by Ric Averill

CHARACTERS

RACHEL: Enthusiastic and cheery, 17.
ANNIE: Her shy, intelligent sister, 15.
TRISH: Their rather forthright friend.
JENNY: A sixties love child.

TIME: The present.
PLACE: A bedroom.

AT RISE: *RACHEL enters the room, followed closely by ANNIE.*

RACHEL. I have to get a haircut.
ANNIE. I have to do my homework.
RACHEL. Good. Go for it, but if you're going to insist on quiet again, forget it. Trish and Jenny are coming over.
ANNIE. Oh, God.
RACHEL. Yes?
   (ANNIE scowls.)
   What do you think I should do with my hair, Annie?
ANNIE *(moving to her books)*. Cut it.
RACHEL. Duh. State the obvious.
ANNIE. I have to study.
RACHEL *(flipping through magazines)*. Did you take Mom's *Glamour* that I brought in here?

ANNIE *(not looking up)*. Do I read *Glamour*?

RACHEL. I just thought you might have cut it up for one of your collages.

(TRISH and JENNNY enter.)

TRISH *(taking over the space as JENNY sits down and looks over ANNIE's shoulder)*. Did someone say collage? I am the queen of collage. You have any magazines, Rachel?

RACHEL. I was just looking for one. I think doofus here used it for an art project.

JENNY *(over ANNIE's shoulder)*. I do not understand calculus.

ANNIE. I did not take your *Glamour*, or I should say, Mom's *Glamour* magazine. I don't like *Glamour* magazine.

TRISH. You don't like *Glamour*. What'd you need it for anyway, Rach?

RACHEL. I want to cut my hair and...

TRISH. Good idea. *(Flipping her own.)*

JENNY. Maybe if I cut my hair I'd understand calculus.

ANNIE *(to JENNNY)*. Maybe if you'd quit leaning over my shoulder, Jenny, I'd understand calculus, or at least be able to finish my homework.

TRISH. I did all my homework in class. *(To RACHEL.)* So what do you want to do with it?

RACHEL. Cut it.

TRISH. Duh.

JENNY. Long hair gives strength. What, Delilah told you your hair needed to be cut?

RACHEL. Steven.

TRISH. Oh, no. Defining our lives by what the boyfriend thinks, are we?

RACHEL. No.

ANNIE. Yes. Always.

RACHEL *(to ANNIE)*. Twit.

JENNY. Just tell him you had it cut. He's a boy. He'll never notice the difference.

TRISH. Brandon would.

ANNIE. Yeah, but he's gay.

TRISH. He is not—well, maybe he is.

JENNY. Shouldn't make judgments.

ANNIE. Just stating facts.

RACHEL. Steven's not gay, and he said he'd take me to the Top of the Tower if I get a fancy haircut.

TRISH. Top of the Tower? Is that like, uh, you know, a euphemism for...

RACHEL. No. It's a restaurant in Kansas City, don't get any ideas.

JENNY. Do you mean he won't take you there if you don't cut your hair?

ANNIE. Double negative, Jenny.

JENNY. I'm never negative.

TRISH. That's kind of crass. I mean, doesn't he like you the way you are?

RACHEL. Yeah, but everybody likes a change.

TRISH. Change boyfriends then.

JENNY. Find one with a different haircut.

ANNIE. Could you guys discuss this somewhere else?

RACHEL. I'm gonna call him. If he doesn't want to date this hair, then he doesn't want to date me.

JENNY. Right on, sister.

TRISH. Liberation triumphs. *(Notices a magazine in the corner.)* Hey, is this the *Glamour* you were looking for?

RACHEL. Yes. See, where it's marked.

(JENNY hops up and they all look.)

JENNY. Awesome.

TRISH. That's a great cut.

RACHEL. Don't you think so? I love it.

ANNIE. Brother.

RACHEL. Come on to the kitchen. I gotta make a call.

TRISH. You gonna tell Steven where to get off?

RACHEL. Heavens, no. I'm gonna call The Hair Connection and get an appointment.

JENNY. Top of the Tower?—maybe we could double date.

TRISH. Or triple.

(They leave the room. ANNIE looks up, closes her book.)

ANNIE. I hate calculus.

BLACKOUT

WAY OF THE WORLD
by Max Bush

CHARACTERS

SARAH: 17
MOLLY: Sarah's sister, 17.
MOTHER: Their mother, 40.
IAN: Molly's former boyfriend, 22.

TIME: Present.
PLACE: The kitchen.

MOLLY died five years ago. IAN has come home from college to see SARAH and also to ask questions about the last day of MOLLY's life. At times, both the past and the present run concurrently, with SARAH switching instantly from five years ago to the present and back again.

IAN. Hey! I brought you something! Where's my manners?
SARAH. You brought me something?
IAN. I brought you something you like.
(He moves to the refrigerator.)
   You were the one who got me started on this stuff. Now I can't stop. It's like a drug. I got to have my ...
(He takes out of bag a half-gallon of:)
BUTTER PECAN ICE CREAM.

110

SARAH. My favorite! You remember!

IAN. I am a man of memory.

SARAH. But how wicked do you feel?

IAN. Very wicked.

SARAH *(holding up a jar)*. Marshmallow topping wicked?

IAN. Oh, yes, yes, yes!

SARAH. And— *(Holding up a jar.)* Mandarin oranges!

IAN. I love mandarin oranges on my ice cream, though I've never had it before.

(She gets a bowl, scoop and spoons while he opens box.)

These are the kinds of things you learn in high school that they just don't teach you in college.

(She puts down the bowl, hands him the scoop.)

What is this? It's a lack of imagination, a lack of real desire; conventionalism without creativity; a recipe for a dull palate, a dull soul. Which is to say: It-is-not-you. *(He tosses scoop aside.)*

SARAH *(pleased how this came out)*. Oh. Thank you.

IAN. My scholarship, if you remember, was in the Science of Consumerism. *(He removes entire block of ice cream, drops the block into the bowl.)* and Behavior Disorders, that is to say, staying up all night eating bizarre foods with other bizarre people.

SARAH. There's hope for me in college.

IAN. Correct. Enticing preparation of food is half the enjoyment. *(Spooning marshmallow on ice cream.)* Anticipation rises, the mouth waters, breathing quickens,

(She dumps the bottle of mandarin oranges in the bowl.)

passions grow, building on one another, *(Stirring with spoon.)* torturing the mind and body, *(Spooning up a large amount.)* until: I must have it! *(He eats. He smiles, moans. Through the food:)* And there it is: A bowl of College Soup.

SARAH. *I must have it! (Takes a large spoonful, eats.)*

IAN. You see? Have it. Have it all!

SARAH. I feel so ... bizarre.

IAN. This is what the best moments of higher education are like.

SARAH *(eating).* Will eating this make me smarter?

IAN. It may make you happier ... for a while. Floating in a sweet cloud of bliss.

SARAH. It tastes good.

IAN. It tastes good. And then college is good. And women are good. I am good.

SARAH. Good grief.

IAN. That too. *(Short silence.)*

SARAH. Why are you here, Ian? How can you just leave college in the middle of the semester?

IAN. I came to see you. I was thinking I wanted to talk to you.

SARAH. About what?

IAN. Molly.

SARAH. What about Molly?

(MOLLY enters, stands and watches.)

IAN. Every year about this time I get a little crazy.

SARAH *(amazed he experiences something similar).* So do I.

IAN. Tell me again when you last saw her.

(MOTHER enters. She "fixes a sandwich.")

SARAH. When I came in for supper, my dad was still at work, my mother was standing by the table and Molly was standing there.

(MOTHER and MOLLY move to the places indicated. IAN and SARAH stop eating ice cream. The following interwoven exchanges move back and forth without pause or light changes. No characters freeze; they should continue to play whichever reality they are in.)

— MOLLY. Why?

— MOTHER. You gave me your word.

IAN. Go on.

SARAH. It will only depress you, don't you think?

IAN. I never really listened to it before. I just want some clear pictures in my mind, I think it will help me.

SARAH. Help you what?

IAN. Understand. To make decisions.

SARAH. What is there to understand. Some drunk ran a stop sign and killed her. You can't understand. There isn't anything to understand because it doesn't make sense.

— MOLLY *(to MOTHER)*. But we can do it tomorrow night. *(Putting her arm around SARAH.) You* can, can't you Sarah? *(Intensely.)* Say yes.

— SARAH. If you take me with you tonight.

— MOLLY *(to MOTHER)*. She can't come with me tonight. I'm going with Ian.

— SARAH. I like Ian.

— MOLLY. Ian is my boyfriend. You're too young and we'll be back too late.

— SARAH. I'm a preteen.

— MOLLY. Wow.

— SARAH. I'm eighty-four in dog years.

— MOLLY. Bow-wow.

— SARAH. And I've become a woman.

— MOLLY. Which is the biggest reason you're not going!

— MOTHER. I don't know if anybody is going anywhere.

SARAH. You see? It doesn't make sense.

— MOTHER. We had a date, Molly.

— SARAH. Yeah, we had a date.

IAN. *We* had a date.

SARAH. If you try to ask, why did this happen—why her, she was just a kid, she didn't do anything wrong, she never did anything to deserve this, her mother loved her, her father loved her, her sister loved her, her friends, her boyfriend loved her—what kind of answer is there that you can understand? It was just luck. If she would have left three seconds earlier or two seconds later, if she hadn't come back to kiss my mother, if that guy had gone down any other street in the whole country. It could happen to anybody, and it does. And what's that? It's the world. You're driving yourself to your boyfriend's house, listening to the radio, and then you're dead. How can you protect yourself against bad luck like that? How can you understand it?

IAN. What were you thinking that day?

SARAH. I wasn't thinking anything except I wanted to go with her. Nothing was different. It was just like any other Friday night.

— MOTHER. And I've been looking forward to it all week. We were going shopping, then bowling and then rent a movie and have a slumber party.

— MOLLY. I'm sorry, we just heard about it today.

— MOTHER. What exactly is it?

— MOLLY. This artist guy has a barn and he decorated it with all his artwork, and tonight he's having a live band there for the grand opening and Ian really, really wants to go.

IAN. Yeah, I did.

— MOTHER. Do you?

— MOLLY. Yes.

IAN. She was going because I wanted to go. If she had stayed with your mother that night—

SARAH. You couldn't have known. People just assume that somehow, something would have told us what was going to happen, but we didn't have any idea. We knew for years my dad was sick, so we were thinking about him, but no one was looking at Molly like that.

IAN. I know I wasn't.

— SARAH. Mom, can I go?

— MOTHER. No!

— SARAH. I'm more of an artist than Molly or Ian.

— MOLLY. She said no, Sarah.

— SARAH. They're just going for the party. I could talk to that guy about art; I could learn something.

— MOTHER. Who would be driving?

— MOLLY. I'm driving to Ian's and then, I don't know, we'll take his truck. *(Silence.)*

— MOTHER *(to MOLLY)*. I'll miss you.

— MOLLY. Thanks, Mom! Thank you, thank you.

— SARAH. You see her every day!

— MOTHER. I'm sorry, but I will. I wanted a date with both my girls.

— MOLLY. We'll have our date tomorrow and then I won't feel bad all night. *(Embracing her.)*

— MOTHER *(holds out keys)*. Take my car, and you drive, not Ian.

— MOLLY *(getting her own keys off wall)*. I can take my car.

— MOTHER. No. I know if you take my car you won't drink or anything. I like Ian, but I don't know, he's too much like your dad. I trust you.

(MOLLY takes keys, starts to go.)

    What about supper?

— MOLLY (keeps going). I'll pick something up on the way.

— MOTHER. Take some of this with you.

— MOLLY *(comes back, takes the "sandwich" from MOTHER)*. Thanks for understanding, Mom. *(She begins to exit, stops, returns, hugs and kisses her MOTHER, then exits the scene.)*

IAN. Then I went looking for her.

SARAH. You don't have to tell me what you found. I saw the pictures.

(MOTHER exits.)

IAN. Shocked ...

SARAH. Yeah.

IAN. No, I mean her face; not serene or calm. She looked shocked.

SARAH. Yeah.

IAN. Like it wasn't supposed to happen.

SARAH. But that's not how the world works. *(Silence.)* So, do you understand something, now?

IAN. No.

SARAH. And you're depressed, aren't you?

IAN. Yeah.

SARAH. So am I.

IAN. And then, your dad died, too.

SARAH. Yeah, two years later.

IAN. God, Sarah, what do you do with all that? How do you—when you feel like this, what do you do?

SARAH. What do *you* do?

IAN. You don't want to know what I do. Did you and your mother change after she was killed?

SARAH. We were like this before she died. But *(Smiling.)* now we're worse.

IAN. So you don't see yourself one way before she died, then another since?

SARAH. No, just more of what I was. But now I'm afraid; I have to hurry up and do what I want to do before someone kills me.

IAN. Yeah.

SARAH. I might be stranger, now.

IAN. How?

SARAH. I don't know. I wear strange clothes, I paint things on my face.

IAN. Why?

SARAH. I like to. If I don't dress the way I feel I get sick to my stomach. And... *(After moment.)* It's a warning. So people know I'm weird. If I don't tell them, then they won't expect it and I'll say something and hurt their feelings. That would break my heart. And the more I dress up, the more I feel like Sarah. I think: I can do this. I can be whoever I want.

IAN. And everybody just loves you for it.

SARAH. No. *(She laughs).* They think I'm evil.

IAN. They hurt you. But you're so afraid of hurting them.

SARAH. Someday, when I have all my supernatural powers, I'll walk around and change them, saying: You are a penguin, you are a hawk, you are a star, you are a spring lily. *(Lying down.)* And then I will lay down in the mud and crocuses will grow out of my dress. I'll look up into the stars, and see myself, floating away.

IAN. I want to be with you that day.

SARAH. Really?

BLACKOUT

HOAGY FREDMEISTER
by *Mark Plaiss*

CHARACTERS

SHERRY: Middle-age mother.
SHERMAN: Middle-age father.
KAREN: Their teenage daughter.
SHELDON: Their teenage son.
UNCLE DICK: Sherman's brother.
FRED HOAGMEISTER: Karen's fiancé.

TIME: The present.
PLACE: A hospital room.

AT RISE: *SHERRY is lying in hospital bed.*

SHERRY *(to offstage).* ...not Platt, *Plate!* I'm Mrs. *Plate!*

(Enter SHERMAN.)

SHERMAN. I am not late.
SHERRY. Sherman! Oh, Sherman! I've got wonderful news! The doctor just...
SHERMAN. We have to talk, Sherry.
SHERRY. ...told me I don't have cancer!
SHERMAN. Fine—
SHERRY. I have a severe facial tic, that's all.
SHERMAN. Great—

119

SHERRY. I'll just twitch a little bit now and then.

SHERMAN. Swell. Now look. Karen's getting married. Married! What are we going to do about that?

SHERRY *(surprised)*. Karen's getting married? When—

SHERMAN. To some guy named Hogmeister, or...

SHERRY. *Hogmeister?*

SHERMAN. ...something like that. A cotton swab salesman, I think...

SHERRY. A what?

SHERMAN. ...from Gnaw Bone, Indiana. Now how is...

SHERRY. When did this all come...

SHERMAN. ...this twenty-year-old, cotton swab salesman gonna provide for our Karen?

(Enter KAREN.)

KAREN *(rushing to greet SHERRY)*. Mother! Oh, Mother! *(They embrace.)* I have the greatest news!

SHERMAN. Hey!

KAREN. I'm going to get married!

SHERMAN *(a little louder)*. Hey!

KAREN. Isn't that wonderful, Mother!

SHERMAN *(a little louder)*. Hey!

KAREN. His name is Fred—

SHERMAN *(louder, still)*. HEY!

KAREN & SHERRY *(turning to SHERMAN)*. WHAT?!

SHERMAN *(to KAREN, calmly)*. Show a little respect for your mother, young lady. The doctor has just given us some fabulous news. Your mother...

SHERRY *(to KAREN)*. I don't have cancer!

(SHERRY and KAREN squeal and hug.)

SHERMAN. ...just has a facial tic...

SHERRY. I'm going to be all right!

SHERMAN. ...really, just a lot of twitching and jerking—

SHERRY. Now, tell me about this boy.

SHERMAN. Yes! What about this boy?

(Enter SHELDON.)

SHELDON. I'm *not* a boy.

SHERRY. Sheldon, your sister's getting married!

SHERMAN *(to KAREN)*. What's his name, anyhow?

SHELDON *(walking over by his mother)*. Hi, Mom.

KAREN. His name...

SHERRY *(to SHELDON, kisses his cheek)*. Hi, sweetie.

KAREN. ...is Fred...

SHERMAN *(to SHELDON)*. Your mom's not going to die.

KAREN. ...Hoag...

SHELDON *(to SHERRY)*. That's great, Mom.

SHERMAN *(to KAREN)*. Who?

KAREN. Fred...

SHELDON *(to SHERRY)*. What ya got, then?

KAREN. ...Hoag...

SHERRY. Just a facial...

KAREN. ...meister.

SHERRY. ...tic.

(Enter UNCLE DICK.)

UNCLE DICK. A tick? Put you in the hospital because of a tick? Never heard of such a thing.

KAREN. Uncle Dick! I've got great news!

UNCLE DICK. Got that tick removed, did ya? Buggers suck the blood—

SHERMAN *(takes UNCLE DICK by shoulders, points to SHERRY)*. *Facial* tic.

UNCLE DICK *(to SHERRY)*. Cherry, how they treating ya?

SHERRY. It's *Sherry*, not Cherry! *(To SHERMAN.)* Twenty-five years and still your brother messes up my name!

UNCLE DICK *(walks over to SHERRY, examines her face)*. Hell, I'd get another doctor. I don't see no tick. *(To SHERMAN.)* Thought it was cancer, Sherm?

SHERMAN. It's a *facial* tic. A neurological condition.

UNCLE DICK. No cancer? That's cause for a celebration!

KAREN. That's me! That's me!

UNCLE DICK. Your don't have cancer or ticks, either?

KAREN. I'm getting married!

SHERRY *(to KAREN)*. Honey, what's this boy's name, again?

KAREN. His name...

UNCLE DICK. Hey, Sheldon. What's a tic?

KAREN. ...is Fred...

SHELDON. A lot of twitching and jerking, I think.

UNCLE DICK *(to SHERMAN)*. What's his name?

SHERMAN. Ted something.

KAREN. Not Ted, *Fred*! Fred Hoag—

SHELDON *(looking intently at MOTHER)*. Mom, do you think...

UNCLE DICK. Fred *Hog*?

KAREN. *Hoag*. Long "O," OK? Fred Hoag...

SHELDON. ...now I don't want you to take this the wrong way or anything...

SHERMAN. Fred Hoag? I don't know—

KAREN *(aggravated)*. No! Not Fred Hoag! Fred Hoag—

SHELDON. ... but do you think it would help ...

UNCLE DICK. *Hoagy? (Begins singing "Star Dust," botches lyrics.)*

SHELDON. ... your facial tic, I mean ...

KAREN *(frustrated)*. Not Hoagy Carmichael!

SHELDON. ... if I reared back ...

KAREN. It's FRED HOAGMEISTER!

SHELDON. ... and punched you right in the jaw?

UNCLE DICK *(loudly and proud, thinking he's figured it out)*. HOAGY FREDMEISTER!

KAREN *(completely frustrated)*. AHHH!

SHERMAN *(thoughtfully)*. I knew a Fred Hoffmeister.

SHERRY. Wasn't he a math teacher at high school?

SHERMAN. No, that was Ted Groghleiter.

(KAREN starts crying. Phone rings. SHELDON picks up.)

SHELDON *(into phone)*. Hello?

UNCLE DICK *(to SHERMAN)*. No, *that* was Ned Feister.

SHERMAN. Who was Ted Groghleiter, then?

SHELDON *(into phone)*. Hold on. *(To SHERRY.)* Mom, it's Grandma.

UNCLE DICK. He taught metal shop.

SHERMAN. That's right.

SHERRY *(to SHELDON)*. Tell her I'm busy and I'll call her back. *(To KAREN.)* Now, baby, who's this Fred Hogmeister's parents?

SHELDON *(into phone)*. Grandma, she's busy—

SHERRY. HOAGMEISTER! HOAGMEISTER! IT'S FRED HOAGMEISTER!

SHELDON *(to SHERRY)*. Mom, Grandma's worried about her cat.

KAREN *(crying)*. I want Fred!

UNCLE DICK. Ed who?

SHERRY *(to UNCLE DICK)*. It's *Fred*, you imbecile!

UNCLE DICK. Who's Fred?

SHERRY. Her fiancé!

UNCLE DICK. Thought that was Hoagy whatshisname?

SHELDON *(still holding phone; to SHERRY)*. Mom, what about Grandma's cat?

SHERRY *(to SHELDON)*. Tell her I'll call her back!

KAREN *(crying)*. I want Fred!

SHERMAN *(to KAREN)*. What church they go to, honey?

SHELDON. Mom, Grandma's pretty upset about the cat. She says—

SHERRY *(shouting, trying to be heard over the phone)*. I DON'T HAVE TIME RIGHT NOW, MOTHER! I'LL CALL YOU BACK!

UNCLE DICK. I would have sworn she said Hoagy Fredmeister.

SHELDON *(to SHERRY)*. Mom, Grandma wants to know if you'll call her back?

SHERRY. Ahhhhhhhh!

UNCLE DICK. That tick flaring up, Cherry?

SHELDON *(into phone)*. Grandma, she'll call you back. *(Hangs up phone.)*

SHERMAN *(to KAREN)*. Are they from around here, honey?

KAREN *(shouting)*. HIS NAME IS FRED HOAGMEISTER. HE WAS BORN AND RAISED IN CLEVELAND WHERE HIS PARENTS STILL LIVE, AND HE'S EPISCOPALIAN!

UNCLE DICK. Knew an Episcopalian once. Turns out he was Catholic.
(Phone rings. SHELDON answers.)
SHERRY *(jerking phone from SHELDON. Into phone).* Mother, take the damn cat to the vet!

(Enter FRED HOAGMEISTER.)

SHERRY, SHERMAN, SHELDON, UNCLE DICK. WHO ARE YOU?
KAREN *(running to FRED, arms outstretched).* FRED!
FRED *(steps past KAREN, extends hand to shake hands with others).* Hoagmeister. Fred Hoagmeister. Damn glad to meet ya.

BLACKOUT

TOLD HER
by *Silvia Gonzalez S.*

CHARACTERS

MULTIPLE CHARACTERS

TIME: The present.
PLACE: Jail.

Note: *Told Her* was written in response to *Women in Jail*, a television program. A defense for murder was from a wife who said she was always being told what to do by male figures until she exploded and shot her husband.

FEMALE. Her father told her to get his shoes
VOICES. She did
FEMALE. Her father told her to get his food
VOICES. She did
FEMALE. Her father told her to get him a beer
VOICES. She did
FEMALE. Her father told her to make her brother's bed
VOICES. She did
FEMALE. Her father told her who to date
VOICES. She did
FEMALE. Her father told her to miss the prom
VOICES. She did
FEMALE. Her father told her to forget school
VOICES. She did

FEMALE. Her father told her who to marry

VOICES. She did

FEMALE. Her father told her to have many children

VOICES. She did

FEMALE. Her husband told her to get his shoes

VOICES. She obeyed

FEMALE. Her husband told her to get his food

VOICES. She obeyed

FEMALE. Her husband told her to get him a beer

VOICES. She did

FEMALE. Her husband told her to make the children's bed

VOICES. She did

FEMALE. Her husband told her to— *(She brings forward a gun and holds it straight ahead stoically. Sound: Gunshot.)*

VOICES. The warden told her to close the cell door

FEMALE. She did...

BLACKOUT

WHAT'S WRONG WITH HIM?
by Linda Daugherty

CHARACTERS

CRICKET: 12-year-old girl.

TOM: Her 15-year-old brother with Down syndrome.

REESE: 12-year-old boy.

GRAN: Cricket and Tom's grandmother.

TIME: The present.

PLACE: A comfortable living room in Cricket's home.

SETTING: *We see a front door, door to kitchen, portable stereo system, and desk covered with books and papers.*

AT RISE: *In blackout, a snappy 1940s tap song plays. Lights rise on TOM seated on floor center, his back to the audience. He is wearing tails, an oversized top hat which comes down to his ears and tap shoes on his hands. Crawling across the floor, he "taps" with the shoes on his hands. He "taps" up the leg of the desk, across the desk, on the wall, up the wall as high as he can reach and down again. GRAN enters from kitchen and turns down music volume.*

GRAN. Tom? *(He doesn't respond and continues his energetic tapping.)* Tom! *(He continues to tap. GRAN*

128

crosses to him and gently puts her hands on his shoulders.) Thomas ...

(He stops tapping and turns to look at her, proudly holding up his tap shoes.)

TOM. See me, Gran? I dancin'.

GRAN. Yes, and you are one noisy dancing boy.

TOM *(enthusiastically)*. I *guh* dancin' boy!

GRAN. That's right, honey. You dance now. But when Cricket gets home from soccer you'll have to stop tapping and turn off your music. Your sister has to study.

(Distracted, TOM taps shoes and his hands together.)

Tom ... *(Putting her hands on his to stop the tapping.)* Tom, are you listening? Cricket has a big test tomorrow and a science report to finish, so you have to be real quiet. Very, very, *very* quiet. *(She takes tap shoes off his hands and puts them on the floor.)* And shoes go on *feet*, okay?

TOM *(hurriedly cramming his feet into tap shoes)*. Okay! Okay! *(Tapping on each syllable.)* O! O! O! Kay!

(She kisses TOM on the head and exits. TOM turns up the music and taps joyfully around the room. He impulsively picks up a stack of index cards from desk as he taps by. He pretends to read the cards while singing.)

Ol MacDanna hadda farm

E-I-E-I-O

An onna farm he hadda—

(He tears a strip off the edge of an index card. He stops dancing and focuses on tearing cards into strips and then into smaller pieces. He carefully gathers up the pieces and throws them into the air over his head like

confetti. CRICKET, in her soccer uniform, enters through the front door, carrying her backpack.)

CRICKET. Hi, I'm home! Whoa. Too loud, Tom!

(She turns off stereo. TOM throws his arms lovingly around her and kisses her. Preoccupied, CRICKET is not responsive. TOM gathers up the pile of torn index cards.)

TOM. Cricky, see me! Wain! Wain! *(He throws paper in air.)*

CRICKET. Rain...that's right, Tom.

(TOM gathers up paper again.)

TOM. Watch gin. Wain! Wain!

CRICKET. I see, Tom. It's rain.

TOM. See me gin. See me. I dancin... *(He throws paper in the air and tap dances.)* ...in wain.

CRICKET. You're dancing and it's raining. A rain dance. Good, Tom.

TOM. No! No! Dancin' in wain! You dance wid me, Cricky! Dance in wain!

CRICKET. Not now, Tom.

TOM. Watch! See! It wains, o-kay?

CRICKET. Okay, okay.

TOM. It wains on Cricky!

(TOM drops "rain" on CRICKET over and over again. She picks up a piece of torn card and realizes that the "rain" is what is left of her science report written on index cards. She is so angry she cries. GRAN appears in kitchen doorway, not seen by CRICKET and TOM.)

CRICKET *(trying to control her anger and tears)*. Tom... Tom... your *rain*... it's my science report.

(TOM stops throwing paper in air and looks at her intently.)

TOM. Yes. You wan wain gin, Cricky?

CRICKET. It's not *rain*! It's my science report, my speech. You tore it up. You ruined it. These cards are what I was going to say. *Understand?* Now I have to do it all over and I have an English test tomorrow. *(She cries in frustration.)*

TOM *(sympathetically patting her)*. Why cry, Cricky?

CRICKET *(crying)*. Do you know how long I worked on this? Oh, what's it to you?!

TOM *(cheerfully)*. Don' cry, Cricky. *(He jumps away and taps.)* Sing wid me! *(Singing.)*

Ol MacDanna hadda farm

E-I-E-I-O

And onna farm he hadda wain—

CRICKET *(frustrated and losing it)*. Why can't you understand anything?! On the farm he had a cow or a *horse* or a *chicken*?

TOM. No! Wain!

CRICKET *(angrily)*. E-I-E-I-O! Remember?! Then we make the sound of the *animal*... Moo, moo! Cluck, cluck! Can't you understand anything?!

TOM *(picking up her mood and intensity)*. Wain! Wain! I dancin'! I dancin'! Wain! I dancin'! *(Angry and frustrated.)* In...! Wain!

(TOM throws himself on the floor, kicking his tap shoes wildly in anger and frustration. GRAN goes to him and gently holds his feet still. The tapping stops. GRAN

rubs his legs and, after a period of silence, she speaks softly to CRICKET.)

GRAN. I rented "Singing in the Rain" for him. You know...Gene Kelly...singing and dancing...in the rain. *(To CRICKET.)* He just wanted to be Gene Kelly, you see? I'm sorry, honey. I'm so sorry about your report. If you could just see it like he... *(A knock on the front door.)* Oh...oh, dear. Cricket, I think...oh, I think I made a mistake.

CRICKET. What?

GRAN. Oh, dear, this is not a good time.

CRICKET. What do you mean, Gran?

GRAN. Reese's mother called—

CRICKET. Oh, no.

GRAN. —and he wanted to come over and study with you for the English test tomorrow, and I thought—

CRICKET. Can't *anybody* think around here?! I don't ask *anyone* over. I don't want—

(Another knock. GRAN and CRICKET look at each other. Resigned, CRICKET crosses to front door. She turns and gestures for GRAN to take TOM to the kitchen.)

GRAN. Come on, Tom. You're hungry.

TOM. I not.

GRAN. Oh, yes, you're hungry...for a popsicle, okay?

TOM. Okay, I hungry...popsicle. *(Jumps up from floor.)*

GRAN. Tom, help me, please.

(TOM enthusiastically kisses GRAN and helps her up. They exit arm in arm to kitchen. CRICKET collects herself and opens door for REESE.)

REESE *(excited and smiling).* Hi!

CRICKET. Hi.

REESE. My mom called your grandmother.

CRICKET. Yeah, I know.

REESE. So my mom's dropped me off...

CRICKET. Yeah, I see.

REESE *(confused by CRICKET's reactions and getting nervous).* So, uh, we could...study English. She went to Sack and Save...my mom...to shop. She'll come by when she's done.

CRICKET. Great.

REESE. So...should I come in?

CRICKET. Sure. Come on in.

(REESE comes in and stands awkwardly in middle of room.)

REESE. I brought my English book and my old tests.

CRICKET. Great. *(She closes door to the kitchen.)*

REESE. I'm sure your tests have all the right answers anyway. Well, it shouldn't be too hard. Mrs. Alcart's tests are pretty easy.

CRICKET. Yeah, should be easy.

REESE. At least for you. I wish I had your brain.

(TOM bursts through kitchen door, wearing his top hat but not his tails. He has a half-eaten, dripping, red popsicle in one hand and another still in the wrapper in the other hand. TOM's mouth, hands and front of his shirt are stained red. GRAN appears a moment later,

*obviously trying to keep up with him. She carries
TOM's tails.)*

TOM. I ga red popsicle!

GRAN. Tom!

TOM. For you, Cricky! *(TOM hugs and kisses CRICKET,
covering her with popsicle juice. Noticing REESE.)*
Who he?

(CRICKET is frozen with embarrassment.)

GRAN. Oh, that's Cricket's friend, Tom. Come on, we're
going to play a game in the kitchen.

TOM. Wa game? *(Pointing at REESE.)* He play?

GRAN. No. Come on, Tom. I...I have a surprise for you
in the kitchen.

*(TOM continues to stare at REESE. GRAN taps TOM
on the shoulder.)*

   Come on, Tom. I have a big, big, *big* surprise in the
kitchen, okay?

TOM. O-kay! *(Runs off to kitchen.)*

GRAN. Hello, Reese. I'm Cricket's grandmother.

(She offers her hand to REESE. He shakes it politely.)

REESE. Nice to meet you.

GRAN *(hanging TOM's tails on the coat rack).* I'm so
glad...we're so glad you could come over and we'll try
not to disturb you again. I'll be in the kitchen if you
need me. *(Exits.)*

REESE *(nervously thumbing through an old test).* So...
uh...I guess Mrs. Alcart'll ask us to do some stupid
diagraming. *(He looks at CRICKET, wishing he hadn't
used the word "stupid.")* I mean—

CRICKET. So, I guess you'll be telling everyone.

REESE. What?

CRICKET. About my "stupid" brother.

REESE *(nervously)*. Oh, he's your brother? I...I didn't know you had a brother. *(Pause.)*

CRICKET. Well, go on. Ask.

REESE *(innocently)*. What?

CRICKET. Oh, please!

REESE *(tentatively)*. So...what's wrong with him?

CRICKET. Don't you listen in science?

REESE. Yeah. Actually, no. Not too much.

CRICKET. My brother has Down syndrome. He's a genetic mistake. Remember, chromosomes? *Hel-lo?* He's a mistake—a stupid mistake! A bunch of stupid brain cells and I'm stuck with him—a mutant!

REESE. I'm...I'm sorry...I didn't know.

CRICKET. And I don't have my stupid science report done because he tore it up! My stupid brother tore it up to make rain!

REESE. I...I—

CRICKET. Can't you think of anything to say? You'll have a lot to say at school tomorrow, I bet, Mr. Reese's Pieces! "Cricket's brother is a retard, a stupid, stupid retard—drooling, talking like a moron!" Right?

REESE *(crams tests into his backpack)*. I...I wouldn't do that...I wouldn't say—

CRICKET. Oh, yeah?! Why?! 'Cause you're so sweet?! Don't come over here ever again! Don't talk to me! Don't ever ask me to a stupid movie again! Understand?! *(Pushing REESE out the front door.)* I hate you, Reese! I hate you! *(CRICKET slams the door shut.)*

BLACKOUT

WELCOME TO MCDONALD'S
by *Michael Schneider*

CHARACTERS

Multiple characters up to a total of 11. They are young people of various ages and gender.

TIME: The present.
PLACE: A McDonald's restaurant.

Note: Slash (/) mark indicates when next speaker starts overlapping.

SCENE 1

PAT. Welcome to McDonald's, may I take your order, please?

SANDY. Gimme two cheeseburgers, a doubleham, small fries, large Coke, small choc shake and an apple pie, to go.

PAT. All right, two hams, double cheese, small fries/

SANDY. No, I said two cheeseburgers, doubleham, small fries, large Coke/ small choc shake and an apple pie, to go.

PAT. OK OK OK. I got it. You want two cheeseburgers.

SANDY. Yup.

PAT. A doubleham.

SANDY. Yup.

PAT. Small Coke, large fries/ small choc shake and an apple pie, to go.

SANDY. Small fries, large Coke.

PAT. What?

SANDY. Small fries, large Coke.

PAT. Right, that's what I said.

SANDY. No, you said small Coke, large fries, it's the other way around.

PAT. Right.

SANDY. I know it's right, it's what I said, but it's not what you said.

(BILLY enters.)

BILLY. Is there a problem here?

PAT. No, I can handle it.

BILLY. It doesn't sound that way, it sounds like there's a problem.

PAT. No,/ it's no big deal

SANDY. Yes, there is. There is a problem.

BILLY. May I help you?

SANDY. Yes! Thank you!

(PAT exits.)

BILLY. OK, what'll you have?

SANDY. I want two cheeseburgers, a doubleham, small fries, large Coke, small choc shake and an apple pie, to go.

BILLY. Well, that's pretty simple—two hams, doublecheese, small fries/

SANDY. Nooooo! *(Pause.)* Two cheeseburgers, a doubleham.

BILLY. Really?

SANDY. Yes!

BILLY. OK, fine. You changed your mind. No problem.

SANDY. I never changed my mind. It's what I wanted when I walked in.

BILLY. Well, I'm sure you know what you want, but I'm not so sure you know what you said.

SANDY. Just gimme a hamburger.

BILLY. What?

SANDY. I'm hungry. Here's five dollars. Gimme a hamburger, gimme anything off the shelf. Keep the change.

BILLY. There's no call to be rude. No one here was rude to you.

(SANDY exits as BOBBY enters.)

SCENE 2

BILLY. Welcome to McDonald's, may I take your... oh... what do you want?

BOBBY. You're being rude. *(Pause.)*

BILLY. Are you gonna order?

BOBBY. You gonna buy me something?

BILLY. No, get outta here.

BOBBY. Whoa! You can't talk rude to the customers.

(ALEX enters.)

BILLY. If you make me lose my job, I'll kill you.

BOBBY. It might be worth it. I think maybe I'll turn around and tell the whole restaurant that you leave big, disgusting goobers of toothpaste in the sink every time you brush your scummy teeth.

BILLY *(over BOBBY's shoulder to ALEX)*. May I help you?

ALEX *(to BOBBY)*. Have you finished?

BILLY. Yeah, s/he's all taken care of—

BOBBY *(to ALEX)*. Yeah, sure, go ahead.

ALEX. OK. Thanks. Uh, I'll have a double cheeseburger, large fries and a small Coke.

BILLY. That for here or to go.

ALEX. Here.

BILLY. OK, that'll be $4.17 with the tax.

(ALEX pays.)

Your change is eighty-three cents. Be back in a minute. *(To BOBBY.)* You can leave now. *(BILLY exits to get ALEX's order.)*

ALEX *(to BOBBY)*. My sister does that.

BOBBY. What?

ALEX. The toothpaste goobers in the sink. Know what I do?

BOBBY. What?

ALEX. I use *her* toothbrush to shove them down the drain.

BOBBY *(referring to BILLY)*. S/he'd kick my butt it I did that.

ALEX. S/he wouldn't have to know, would s/he?

BOBBY *(seeing the light)*. No, s/he wouldn't. *(Pause.)* Gee, thanks. *(To BILLY, who has returned.)* Bye, don't spill the fries.

BILLY. Bye, don't come again. *(Handing ALEX the bag.)* Here, you're all set. Have a nice day.

ALEX. Thanks. You, too.

SCENE 3

(ALEX goes to a table and starts eating. GUS sits at another table and accidentally knocks his cup to the floor. RONNY, an employee, begins to pick it up.)

GUS. Don't touch that!

RONNY. What?

GUS. Leave it alone.

RONNY. Why?

GUS. It's your own stupid rule.

RONNY. Hunh? What are you talking about?

GUS. Read it. Right here. What does it say?

RONNY *(reading).* "Please put litter in its place." That's what I'm trying to do.

GUS. Well, it can't be done, can it?

RONNY. What's the matter with you?

GUS. With me? Nothing. The problem is with you and all the other 250 million ignorant, complacent, illiterate and illogical boobies in this country.

RONNY. Thank you. Look, I'm just trying to do my job.

GUS. Aren't you though. Follow orders, do what you're told, never question, never think. My job is much harder. I'm trying to awaken you out of your mental torpor. This exhortation to put litter in its place is absurd. You might as well say, "Please put the sky in its place, please put the corner in its place, please put the end in its place." Litter is defined by place. Now, if litter is unwanted in this establishment, they should say, "Please pick up litter. Cause it to become non-litter" but not "Please put litter in its place." Litter's place is on the ground.

RONNY. You mean like this!

(Knocks GUS' fries onto the floor, starts to walk away as GUS splutters protests, then turns.)

I wouldn't eat that if I were you. It's LITTER!

(GUS is nonplused; stares catatonically at the spilled fries.)

SCENE 4

PHIL *(carrying a book bag, joins ALEX at his table)*. So, like this dog, this like pit bull, pukes right on my book bag!

ALEX. This book bag?

PHIL. Yeah.

ALEX. Whoa, yuck, get it off the table!

PHIL. I cleaned it up, most of it, you can hardly tell, just a little bit around the stitching.

ALEX. Get it off!

PHIL. All right! Jeez, no big deal. There, you happy now? Can we go on? *(Pause, no answer.)* Where was I? Oh yeah, well, like you could see everything, all the parts of the chicken, you know, the feathers, part of the head, he like musta swallowed chunks of it, you could even see bits of corn from the chicken's stomach.

ALEX *(pushes food away)*. Why are you doing this? You think it's funny?

PHIL. What?

ALEX. You're making me sick. You're making everyone around us sick. *(ALEX looks around.)* And you're embarrassing me.

PHIL. I'm sorry.

ALEX. I can't eat now. You made me waste $4.17.

PHIL. I said I'm sorry. Let's just change the subject, let's talk about ... uh ... like ... uh ... uh ... you really not going to eat the rest of that?

ALEX. No!

PHIL. Well, can I have it?

(Reaches for hamburger, ALEX gets up and exits.)

SCENE 5

(ALEX encounters CHRIS on the sidewalk out front.)

CHRIS. Excuse me, could I have just one moment of your time? *(Hands ALEX a card.)*

ALEX *(reading card).* "I'm a beggar. Give me a dollar and I'll go away." I don't get it.

CHRIS *(takes card back).* What don't you understand?

ALEX. You're a beggar?

CHRIS. Yes I am.

ALEX. You're wearing a suit.

CHRIS. I'm a very successful beggar.

ALEX *(laughs).* Well, not with me you're not. *(Tries to walk on.)*

CHRIS *(intercepting him).* I wouldn't do that if I were you.

ALEX. Are you threatening me?

CHRIS. Oh, no no no. That's such an ugly word. I'm advising you. I know having to pay me a dollar is pretty irritating—I'd hate it myself—but believe me, it's far less irritating than going shopping with me for the next hour.

ALEX. Well, I'm going to walk straight to the nearest policeman.

CHRIS. And tell him what?

ALEX. I'll tell what you're doing.

CHRIS. That's been tried. It never works. He'll just think you're a wacko.

ALEX. I'll show him the card.

CHRIS. What card?

ALEX *(realizes he doesn't have it)*. He'll search you.

CHRIS. No policeman is going to search a well-dressed person such as myself on the word of someone who looks like you searching for a business card. Get real.

ALEX. I don't believe this is happening. *(Walks on rapidly.)*

CHRIS *(keeping pace)*. Where to first? I think you need new shoes for starters.

(JACKY enters the scene, looks up in the air and screams.)

JACKY. Oh, no!

(ALEX looks up, too.)

CHRIS *(to ALEX)*. What a sucker. No one falls for that gag anymore!

(ALEX and JACKY keep looking up, restaurant crowd comes out onto the sidewalk and looks up, ad-libs various questions and exclamation. CHRIS finally looks up.)

Oh, probably just some people shooting a commercial.

(SAM enters.)

SAM. What's everybody looking at?

JACKY. There's a woman up there, on a window ledge/

SAM *(looks up, spots woman, yells)*. JUMP!

JACKY. What's the matter with you?

SAM. What's the matter with you?

JACKY. I didn't tell the lady to jump.

SAM. You didn't yell, but that's what you want.

JACKY. I do not.

SAM. Well, let's go then.

JACKY. Hunh?

SAM. Let's go. If you really don't want her to jump, you certainly don't want to see her jump, so let's get out of here before she does. Watching her stand on the ledge isn't especially interesting.

JACKY. But...uh. Don't you care?

SAM. Care? No I don't care, and neither do all these other people, they just wanna see her jump.

JACKY. I don't believe you.

SAM. Why should I have feelings of involvement in some total stranger's suicide? Just because I chose to walk down Clinton instead of St. Paul? Come on. Let's get out of here. Under the facade of concern on all these faces lurks the heart of a bloodthirsty mob.

JACKY. No, wait. There's a fireman climbing out the window.

SAM. Oh well, now it's more interesting. We have a drama. We have suspense. Will he get there in time? Will he succeed? Will he knock her off? Will she knock him off? Will they both fall off? Will they kill members of this bloodthirsty mob when they hit?

JACKY. You're WEIRD!

(Crowd suddenly gasps; SAM looks up just before he gets hit by the falling woman.)

BLACKOUT

TEAMPLAY
by *John O'Brien*

CHARACTERS

COACH: Man (or woman), mid-30s.
JANET:
CHRISTINE:
MARIE: } Students, all members of a cross-country running team. In their teens.
KIM:
SHERRY:

TIME: The present.
PLACE: A locker room.

AT RISE: *The team is in a happy, relaxed mood. When the COACH enters, the mood becomes tense.*

COACH. Don't get dressed. Nobody gets dressed yet. No showers. No boyfriends. No autographs. No nothing. Just sit down. Did you hear me? Does anybody listen to me? *(The girls sit.)*
All right. What did I say, just before the race? Somebody tell me. Any volunteers? Janet? You just broke the league record on this course. You should know something. What did I say before the race?
JANET. You said to take it easy today.
COACH. But you didn't take it easy, did you? Did you?
JANET. No.

145

COACH. Nobody took it easy. Five runners ran the best times of their careers. You won a two-mile race by four hundred yards. Why did you do it? Any volunteers? Christine?

CHRISTINE. We just felt like running. It's such a beautiful day. Once we got into the woods, it was all so lovely, with leaves turning red and yellow.

COACH. Are you a poet or a runner?

CHRISTINE. I was just trying to explain what happened.

COACH. I know what happened. I want to know whose idea it was.

KIM. It was everybody's idea.

COACH. Five bodies, one mind?

KIM. Something like that.

COACH. Sounds mystical.

MARIE. It was.

COACH. I know my problem. I use words when I talk. I should get a blanket and a book of matches and send smoke signals. Let me go over it again, now that it's too late to undo what you've done. You were running today against a weak opponent. They had no chance to beat you. Next week you run against a strong opponent, with a very good chance to beat you. Under these circumstances, what should your strategy be? That's where I come in. That's why they call me Coach. You do the running. I do the thinking. When I woke up this morning, I had it all figured out. It's the first race of the season. Nobody knows how good you are. So today, you sprint into the woods until you are out of sight of the opposing team. Then you run at three-quarters speed until they catch up with you. At that point, you sprint out of the woods to the finish line. You win the race, but your times are slow, and our next week's opponent won't train hard because of overconfidence. That was the way it was supposed to be, but that's not the way it is. Now everybody knows how good you are, and our next week's opponent will be ready for us. And you tell me the leaves are changing. If you want to see the leaves change, turn in your uniform and buy a book on botany.

MARIE. Coach?

COACH. Somebody knows my name.

MARIE. I was thinking...

COACH. That's a mistake.

MARIE. Isn't this a sport?

COACH. What are you trying to say?

MARIE. Aren't we supposed to be learning sportsmanship? Sportswomanship?

COACH. Let me know when you go to law school. I'll write you a recommendation.

JANET. You didn't answer her question.

COACH. Didn't I?

JANET. I think she's right.

COACH. Do you?

JANET. We all do.

COACH. All?

JANET. Everybody. The whole team.

COACH. Is that true? Sherry?

SHERRY. Yes.

COACH. You need a new coach.

SHERRY. We don't want a new coach.

COACH. I'm no good to you this way.

KIM. We just want to run.

COACH. Your own way.

MARIE. The only way we know.

CHRISTINE. As fast as we can.

MARIE. Every time.

COACH. Where does that leave me? Just a guy holding a stopwatch?

JANET. That leaves you as the coach of a team of girls who love to run and who are too proud to go into the woods and loaf.

COACH. You may lose next week's race.

JANET. If we do, we'll lose to a better team. That's what it's all about.

COACH. All right, take your showers. Don't forget to do your botany homework.

CHRISTINE. Coach?

COACH. Don't call me "Coach." Just say, "Hey, you."

CHRISTINE. I can't do that.

COACH. Try it. It'll grow on you.

CHRISTINE. Is there any practice tomorrow?

COACH. No thanks. On Saturday, I belong to my wife.

CHRISTINE. Excuse us for a minute.

(The girls huddle, whispering to each other. They break the huddle.)

We'd like to invite you and your wife to join us.

COACH. For what?

KIM. A walk in the woods.

MARIE. I'll bring the binoculars.

SHERRY. I'll bring the bird-watching book.

JANET. It's really beautiful out there.

MARIE. Especially in the fall.

COACH. You've done it before?

CHRISTINE. We walk together every weekend.

COACH. Do you really see birds?

JANET. We really do.

COACH. What kind?

JANET. All kinds,

KIM. You name It. We've seen it.

COACH. Baltimore Orioles?

SHERRY. We saw nine of them last week.

CHRISTINE. Name another one.

COACH. Toronto Blue Jays?

MARIE. What do you say, Coach?

COACH. I'll ask my wife.

MARIE. Thanks.

COACH. Think nothing of it. I'm that kind of guy.

JANET. You're our kind of guy.

COACH. Go on. Take your showers. *(Nobody moves.)* Will somebody do something I say?

JANET. Let's go.

(The girls whoop it up as they exit.)

COACH *(calling after them)*. What time tomorrow?

BLACKOUT

THE QUESTION
by Max Bush

CHARACTERS

SARAH: 17.
SALLY: 17, Sarah's friend.
BRANDON: 17, also Sarah's friend.

TIME: Present.
PLACE: The kitchen of Sarah's home.

SARAH's sister MOLLY died five years ago. IAN, MOLLY's former boyfriend, has come home from the university to see SARAH and to try to understand MOLLY's death. In the process, IAN has admitted he quit college and now wants SARAH to join him as he sets out in a camper for the West.

AT RISE: *SARAH, BRANDON and SALLY are returning to Sarah's house after a disastrous rehearsal of the school play,* A Midsummer Night's Dream. *BRANDON and SALLY are worried about SARAH and question her bizarre behavior. All three enter kitchen.*

SARAH. Mom?
BRANDON. What did you mean you may not be in school?
SARAH. Mom?

150

BRANDON. You mean tomorrow?

SARAH. No note again.

BRANDON. What's going on, Sarah?

SARAH. She promised me she'd write me a note.

SALLY. I mean with you.

SARAH. Ian asked me to go with him.

SALLY. When?

SARAH. Tomorrow.

BRANDON. Are you serious?

SALLY. You mean, tomorrow you'd just go?

BRANDON. Quit school, quit the play—

SARAH. You may not have noticed but school and the play are quitting me.

SALLY. What are you thinking, Sarah?

SARAH. I'm thinking of going.

BRANDON. Hasn't anybody else noticed that The Ian was Molly's boyfriend? Isn't this a little strange?

SALLY. Yes it is.

SARAH. Sally!

SALLY. Well it is.

SARAH. You didn't think so before.

SALLY. I didn't know he blew it at school before.

SARAH. I didn't say he blew it. I said he quit.

SALLY. Why is he so interested in you anyway? Why isn't he running away with some girl from college?

SARAH. They're not like him.

SALLY. Dropouts?

BRANDON. I know you're going to tell me this is none of my business—

SARAH. It's none of your business.

BRANDON. —but the way you look, the way you've been acting, I think you're hurting yourself again.

SARAH. You too, Brandon?

BRANDON. Maybe not with pills, but you love to act, you love it more than anything. You're great at it. You would never quit a play.

SARAH. You saw what it's like. How can you be so smart and understand so little?

SALLY. But he's right, you're... you're covering yourself up, you're hiding.

SARAH. I'm not hiding. How can you say that? I'm showing everybody who I am all the time. *You're* hiding. You dress just like everybody else, both of you look like everybody else. That's hiding. *(Beat.)* But that's all right, too. I'm not saying that's bad.

SALLY. That butterfly was like you, but I don't think this is.

BRANDON. I was secretly impressed with that butterfly that you painted on your face. I am often impressed with you, Sarah. You're extremely intelligent; you give me new perspectives on things.

SALLY. Which you need.

BRANDON. Which I need.

SALLY. Because:

BRANDON. I am analytical.

SALLY. Which is:

BRANDON. Dull as dirt.

SALLY. Right. And you're:

BRANDON. Emotional.

SALLY. And that's:

BRANDON. Sexy.

SALLY. So please:

BRANDON. Stay.

SALLY. No, I mean, please:

BRANDON *(getting on his knee).* Stay.

SALLY. NO, I MEAN:

BRANDON *(taking SARAH's hand).* I want to kiss you all over all the time, so please stay.

SALLY. Oh, really, Brandon, we didn't know.

BRANDON. I know we should be together because you and my mother have the same first name.

SARAH. Oh, Brandon...

SALLY. That's so sweet.

SARAH. That's sick.

SALLY. I think it's fate.

SARAH. Sally!

BRANDON. Why do you like that guy, anyway?

"I am as well-derived as he,

As well possess'd; my love is more than his."

(Kisses SARAH's hand.)

SARAH. Ah, Brandon, what are you doing? You kissed my hand! *(She holds her hand up.)* Take it back.

BRANDON. I gave it to you; I want you to have it.

SARAH. What am I supposed to do with this? *(She wipes it off on her bottom.)*

BRANDON. Oh, that's romantic.

SARAH. Stand up. *(He doesn't.)*

BRANDON. It's Molly's day.

SALLY. Yeah, it's this day.

BRANDON. You shouldn't decide anything, today.

SALLY. You haven't told your mother yet, have you? How would she feel?

BRANDON. What's this really about?

SARAH. I have to get ready for Ian.

BRANDON. Is this about your sister?

SARAH. It's about me.

SALLY. It looks like it's about dying.

SARAH. It's about living my life if my friends would let me!

BRANDON. How are you going to do that? Do you have any money?

SALLY. Yeah, how are you going to eat?

SARAH. Sally!

SALLY. I can't help it! You look sad! I don't think you really want to do this. And who's going to play your part? Brandon?

(They both glance at BRANDON who smiles weakly.)

SARAH. That's how they did it in Shakespeare's time.

BRANDON *(as a suffering heroine)*.

"Oh spite! O hell! I see you all are bent
to set against me for your merriment."

SALLY. It's Shakespeare, not *Heidi*.

BRANDON *(in a manly voice)*. What is this *Heidi* stuff?

SALLY. And you can't leave me alone with Doug and Matt! They'll put me in jail because I'll have to kill them.

SARAH. You have to go. I have to get ready for Ian.

BRANDON. You don't want to talk about this?

SARAH. Not now.

BRANDON. But you have to talk about this.

SARAH. Not now!

BRANDON *(sitting on floor)*. Yes, now. We may not see you again.

SARAH. I have to be alone and think.

SALLY *(sitting on floor)*. You can think with us here.

BRANDON. We'll listen. Go ahead. Think.

SALLY. Out loud. *(Silence.)* No, out loud.

BRANDON. Sarah, you can think what you want but you have to talk to us before you do anything.

SARAH *(pulling him up, moving him toward door).* Please, you have to go. I really do need to be alone and think.

BRANDON. Will you call me later?

SARAH. I don't know.

SALLY *(firmly staying on the floor).* Then call *me* or I'm not leaving.

SARAH. All right, I'll call you both.

BRANDON. Promise you'll call before you do anything.

SARAH. I promise.

SALLY. Call me!

(BRANDON and SALLY exit.)

BLACKOUT

OFF COURSE
by *Jonelle Grace*

CHARACTERS

SARAH: A 12-year-old girl.
SE: Sarah's self-esteem.
BRAIN: Sarah's brain.

TIME: The present.
PLACE: Inside Sarah's world.

Since her father's death and mother's remarriage, SARAH has been extremely upset but has not expressed those feelings to her family, friends or the counselor at school. As a result, she has begun making some very poor choices. Then one day she wakes from a nap to find SE in her room. SE convinces SARAH to go on a journey inside herself and visit BRAIN, HEART and her EMOTIONS to find out why she is making particular choices. In the following scene, SARAH and SE arrive in SARAH's brain to discover BRAIN busy at work.

SARAH. Wow, is that really my brain?

SE. Yes, amazing, isn't it?

BRAIN *(walking rapidly toward SARAH, carrying a stack of papers toward a box marked "out box")*. Please step aside. Please step aside. Input in progress. Input in progress. Oh, dear, oh dear, wrong box—wrong box— brain complications.

SARAH *(steps aside as BRAIN hurries past)*. I'm sorry, I didn't mean to—

BRAIN. Please stand back. Please! Stand back! Oh, dear, oh, dear, now what was I doing?

SE. Well, what do you think, Sarah?

SARAH. It's all rather complex.

SE. Why don't you take a closer look?

(SARAH moves toward BRAIN.)

BRAIN. If you don't mind, you're beginning to get on my nerves. I have work to do. I'm in charge here, you know. Now, what was I doing?

SARAH. It, uh, it doesn't seem to be too organized.

SE. Yes, well, uh, the part you see right now is what we refer to as the "new" part of the brain. It handles all the short-term memory processes—that sort of thing.

BRAIN. Oh, dear, now what was I just about to do. I wish I could remember.

SARAH. Am I in any danger with, uh, with it being in charge of things?

SE. Yes, well ... what we want to examine first are the messages which you've accumulated in your brain and how these messages affect your ability to make decisions. *(She climbs up to a box with wires sticking out here and there. A computer keyboard is visible.)* Here, you better watch how I do this. It has a mind of its own sometimes. *(Typing a command.)* Let's see now how many messages you've already stored. Oh, my, unbelievable—one million four hundred fifty-two thousand eight hundred and ninety-four. I think perhaps we should narrow the data field. *(She types again.)*

BRAIN. Hey, watch what you're doing! Do you even have a brain? Be careful up there!

SE. I know—we'll just ask for today's messages. *(Types in a command.)* There, that should do it. Well, are you ready?

SARAH. Ready for what?

SE. To hear the messages.

SARAH. I'm actually going to hear them? It's not going to just print them out?

SE. There, it's all set. Go ahead, Sarah. You just have to connect those wires.

(SARAH climbs up to the control box.)

BRAIN. No, wait, don't—

(SARAH connects the wires.)

  Situation #1—interaction with stepfather, Richard—attitude "poor."

BRAIN AS SARAH. Richard—he's such a jerk. I don't know why Mom ever married him. I wish he'd just go away.

SARAH. That's me. That's me talking. *(An alarm sounds.)*

SE. Oh, dear.

SARAH. What's happening?

BRAIN. Warning! Warning! Surface attitude dishonest— evidence of underlying emotional trauma. True feelings are as follows—

(SARAH connects different wires.)

  Data on situation #1 terminated.

SE. I take it there was something there you didn't want to hear.

SARAH. I just want to see what's next—that's all. *(She connects wires.)*

BRAIN. Situation #2—cheating by sharing homework— conflicting messages.

BRAIN AS SHAWNA. Cheating is wrong, Sarah—you'll get us in trouble.

SARAH. That's my best friend, Shawna.

BRAIN AS DAD. People never learn by cheating, Sarah.

SARAH. Dad?

BRAIN AS DANNY. Come on, Sarah, everyone cheats—

SE. That's Danny—right?

SARAH. He just needed help with his math.

SE. So, you let him copy your homework.

BRAIN AS DANNY. By the way, Mike asked if you'd be at the party—

SE. Mike?

SARAH. He's just this boy I kind of like.

SE. And if you helped Danny cheat, maybe he'd put in a good word for you?

BRAIN AS SARAH. I want Mike to like me. I need him to like me.

SE. You again?

SARAH. I guess. *(An alarm sounds.)*

BRAIN. Warning! Warning! Underlying emotional trauma —evidence of a powerful need to be love and accepted. Cause of trauma related to—

(SARAH crosses other wires.)

Data on Situation #2 terminated. I wish you would let me finish what I start. Step aside, step aside.

SE. Something else you don't want to hear?

(SARAH crosses wires.)

BRAIN. Situation #3—issues involving friendship.

BRAIN AS MOM. Why didn't you ride home with Shawna?

SARAH. I told Mom I had a meeting. She didn't believe me.

SE. I see.

BRAIN AS SHAWNA. Nobody could ever have a better friend than you, Sarah.

SE. Shawna again?

SARAH. Yeah. I was supposed to spend the night with her, but—

BRAIN AS MIKE. You think Shawna will cover for you so you can go to the party?

BRAIN AS DAD. There is no greater gift in life than a true friend.

SE. Your dad has a point.

BRAIN AS SARAH. Mike's going to be at the party. Shawna won't care.

SARAH *(crossing wires)*. I said I was sorry!

BRAIN. Data on situation #3 terminated.

SE. So, what happened? Did you decide to go to the party and forget about Shawna?

SARAH. I didn't have to decide. Mom wouldn't let me go.

SE. Why was that?

SARAH. Because I didn't get my room cleaned and—

SE. I thought it was because you lied about staying after school for a meeting when you were really with Mike.

SARAH. No, it wasn't that. I...I don't want to do this anymore. *(Climbing down.)*

SE *(climbs up to control box)*. Why don't we try one more. *(Crosses wires.)*

BRAIN. Situation #4—substance use—alcohol and cigarettes.

BRAIN AS MIKE. Just look around your house. See what you can find.

SARAH. Mike thought my folks might have some beer or vodka or something. I wasn't really going to take anything.

BRAIN AS MIKE. I got you some of the cigarettes you like, Sarah.

SARAH. Okay, I've heard enough.

BRAIN AS MIKE. How 'bout I give you a ride—

SARAH *(turning to BRAIN)*. You can stop. Okay? I don't want to hear any more!

BRAIN. Media input regarding drinking and smoking. These activities are fun—your friends will think you're cool—everyone does it—important people do it. Opposing media input—celebrity testimonial—"If you want to be your best—don't do drugs."

SARAH'S VOICE. What does it matter what I do—nobody cares anyway.

BRAIN. Statistical information gained from personal research in school— There are hundreds of chemical substances in cigarette smoke. Tars damage lung tissue and are the main cancer-causing agent in cigarette smoke. Some of the diseases caused by cigarette smoking are—

SARAH. I know all this. Officer Davis came to our class and—

BRAIN AS OFFICER DAVIS. Alcohol is a chemical depressant drug that slows down the activity of the brain and spinal cord.

SARAH. Stop it. I said stop!

BRAIN AS OFFICER DAVIS. Young people often use alcohol as a way to cope with the changes that occur in their lives. Many drink to get away from problems and deal with frustration and anger—

SARAH *(climbing up to control box. SE steps down).* Why won't he stop? How do you shut it off? *(Frantically looking for wires to cross.)*

SE. Wrong wires, Sarah.

(SARAH picks two wires and starts to cross them.) No, Sarah, not that one!

SE & BRAIN. Don't cross the wires!

BRAIN *(becomes increasingly more frantic).* Warning! Warning! Underlying emotional trauma—extreme confusion—rapid message replay—rapid message replay. System malfunction—system malfunction—messages cannot be terminated—cannot be terminated. *(Alarm continues to sound.)* Overload! Overload! Problem ignored—system shutdown! *(Collapses into the out box.)*

SE. Pretty confusing isn't it? All those messages playing in your mind at once. Makes it kind of hard to make decisions.

SARAH. I guess.

SE. Let me ask you something, Sarah. Do you want to be happy—feel good about yourself?

SARAH. Sure. I mean that's what you want me to say, isn't it?

SE. I want you to be honest. Do you think of yourself as a good person?

SARAH. I don't know.

SE. Well, I think you are, and I know just where we can go to prove it. *(Extends her hand.)* Shall we?

SARAH. It depends on where we're going

SE. Your heart.

SARAH. The heart's just an organ. Everyone knows that.

SE. Oh, no, the heart's a very magical and safe place.

SARAH. If it's so safe, then why do hearts get broken?

SE. Because they care. But, hearts are stronger than you think, Sarah. Come on. Grab hold! We're headed up a major artery!

(SARAH takes SE's hand and the two exit.)

BLACKOUT

MEATBALLS
by Michael Schneider

CHARACTERS

MIRANDA	ELIZABETH
BERNICE	LYDIA
MICHAEL	QUINNE
MARIA	SARAH
CARLOS	BETH
AMY	KATHERINE
ELI	ANNE
ALEXANDRA	NICK
JOE	JASON
KAREN	

TIME: The present.

PLACE: The kitchen and dining room of a small restaurant.

Note: Slash (/) mark indicates when next character starts overlapping.

AT RISE: *We see both the kitchen and dining areas of the restaurant. On the right half of the stage there is a kitchen worktable. MIRANDA and BERNICE are standing at the far ends of it, preparing vegetables, a mixing bowl in the center between them. On the left of the stage there are three small dining tables. MICHAEL is meticulously setting them, carefully measuring the amount of tablecloth overhang on each side, measuring to place the silverware, readjusting, etc. MARIA, Michael's therapist, is supervising. CARLOS enters, passing through the kitchen. He stops abruptly in front of the bowl between MIRANDA and BERNICE.*

CARLOS. Where's Alice?

MIRANDA. Where's Alice?

BERNICE. You mean Alex, Alexandra.

CARLOS. Whatever! Alice Alex the little blond bimbo makes the meatballs. She's late again?

MIRANDA. Uh, yeah, I guess she is—late.

CARLOS *(can't tell if MIRANDA is being smart with him; stammers).* Well... well. *(Pointing with his finger; he can't think of what to say and stomps off.)*

(AMY enters, passing through the kitchen.)

MIRANDA & BERNICE. Hiiii, Aaamy.

AMY *(stops short, looks at the bowl between MIRANDA and BERNICE).* Alexandra's late again!?

MIRANDA & BERNICE. Eeeeyupp!

AMY. Oh no. I am not doing it. I am not mixing those meatballs. I covered for her Tuesday. I finally got the smell off my hands last night.

BERNICE. She'd do it for you.

AMY. Yeah rrrightt! When monkeys fly outta my butt. If Carlos comes in, you didn't see me.

(She exits. ELI enters with large mayonnaise jar.)

MIRANDA & BERNICE. Rrrright!

ELI. How can you tell if mayonnaise has gone bad?

MIRANDA & BERNICE. Go away, Eli.

ELI. No, I'm totally serious.

BERNICE. He's totally serious.

MIRANDA. He's totally serious.

ELI. No, really!

MIRANDA. You know, I'm beginning to think he's totally serious.

BERNICE. He hasn't gone away.

MIRANDA. No, he hasn't.

BERNICE. Well, Eli, why don't you eat about a pound of it and see how you feel in the morning.

ELI. I'm supposed to use it in the Waldorf salad.

MIRANDA (handing ELI a carrot stick). Drop this in. If it sinks about half way it's probably OK.

(ELI takes the carrot, drops it in; they both look at him.)

ELI. It bounced off. (Pause.) I guess that probably means it's bad, hunh?

(They give each other a look, "Duh?!")

I'll try it again. (He takes the carrot out and drops it in again.) This time it broke through, and this like clear, purple liquid is oozing up through the hole. It kinda reminds me/

BERNICE (yelling). Eli, get out of here!

MIRANDA. Go!

(ELI exits. ALEXANDRA enters, in a hurry. She is wearing oversized suit coat, false beard, and top hat.)

ALEXANDRA. Does Carlos know I'm late?

BERNICE. Uh, well, he just stopped and asked if the little blond/ bimbo was here yet.

MIRANDA. Uh, yeah, he noticed.

ALEXANDRA. The what!?

MIRANDA. He couldn't have/ meant you.

ALEXANDRA. What a jerk.

BERNICE. How'd it go?

(*ALEXANDRA kicks a box on the floor.*)

That good, huh?

ALEXANDRA. I sit there for an hour. Then they send out some ditz wannabe to tell me they're so sorry, could I come back Monday.

BERNICE. Carlos's not gonna go for the beard.

MIRANDA. Carlos's mad already.

ALEXANDRA. Carlos can take this lousy/ job and shove—

(*CARLOS enters.*)

CARLOS. She still ain't here. Bernice, get rid of the weirdo friend. You gotta make the meatballs.

ALEXANDRA. Hi, Carlos.

CARLOS. What?

ALEXANDRA. I'll finish the meatballs. I can see you already started them for me. Thanks.

CARLOS. For you? For you I do nothing! I should have my head examined I ever do anything for you.

ALEXANDRA. Well, um—

CARLOS. What's the matter with you? You come half an hour late looking like some kinda transvestite weirdo.

ALEXANDRA. I'm sorry. I had an/ audition. There was no phone.

CARLOS. I don't wanna hear it. Finish the meatballs. Then you're fired.

ALEXANDRA. If I'm fired, pay me.

CARLOS. After the meatballs. And take that off, people can see in here.

(CARLOS yanks the beard off of ALEXANDRA. ALEX-ANDRA screams in pain. CARLOS tosses the beard aside and it lands in the meatball mixing bowl, MI-RANDA and BERNICE following it with their eyes.)

Now get to work. *(He exits.)*

(ALEXANDRA notices BERNICE and MIRANDA star-ing into the bowl; ALEXANDRA looks into the bowl and sees the beard; BERNICE reaches in to take it out.)

ALEXANDRA. Don't touch that!

(BERNICE and MIRANDA look at ALEXANDRA. AL-EXANDRA plunges her hands into the bowl and starts mixing.)

BERNICE. Carlos can't fire you. Joe would have to do that. *(ALEXANDRA keeps mixing.)* You're not really fired.

(ALEXANDRA stops, takes hands out, looks into the bowl, spits in it and goes back to mixing.)

MIRANDA. She is now.

(BERNICE and MIRANDA give up and go back to work. Lights up on the other side of the stage. During the scene that follows, ALEXANDRA finishes the meat-ball mixing and carries the bowl away. BERNICE and MIRANDA also exits.)

MARIA. Michael. You already measured that side. Six times.

MICHAEL. You...have no idea. This...this table isn't square. Those two corners are *(indicating the two downstage corners)* eighty-nine degrees and those two are ninety-one so it's really a trapezoid so on these two sides you have to take an average and measure from the middle and it's your fault you wouldn't let me make a new tablecloth, either that or cut the table, I mean the problem is real, you know, reality, you're always telling me to face reality, well this is real and it's not going to go away just because we don't deal with it.

MARIA. Michael. Start with the knives.

MICHAEL. But—

MARIA. Stop measuring and do the knives. If you don't do the knives, you'll never get to the spoons, forks, napkins, water glasses, flowers, salt and pepper.

(MICHAEL is by now clutching some table knives and acting paralyzed.)

Michael. Place a knife.

(JOE enters.)

JOE. Doc, could I talk to you a minute?

(JOE escorts MARIA downstage. MARIA keeps an eye on MICHAEL and says some of her lines upstage to MICHAEL.)

MARIA. Put it down. Put the knife down. Good.

JOE. You know, Doc, I admire what you're trying to do here but/

MARIA. No! Put the ruler away. Move around the table and place another knife.

JOE. Like I say, I admire what you're trying to do but I don't think it's gonna work.

MARIA. It takes time. Good, Michael. No, put the ruler away. Next, knife.

JOE. Um...it's been three weeks.

MARIA. Un hunh, and he's made a lot of progress. Good. Now the spoons. No. Put the ruler down. Remember, we agreed, no measuring until the forks.

JOE. I can't see it.

MARIA. Can't see what? Good, now place another one.

JOE. The progress.

MARIA. Oh really. Are you an expert? Good, good. Now, another one.

JOE. No.

MARIA. He's gone from ninety-one minutes to forty-eight minutes.

JOE *(deadpan)*. Per table?

MARIA *(joyfully)*. Yes!

JOE. I have a better idea. I'll build a little stage over there, lights, the whole works. Put a table. He can do his thing. Entertainment.

MARIA. What?

JOE. It's a show. Like one of those live exhibits at the museum. The man who sets the table. For an hour. It's unique. My customers will love it.

MARIA. Put the handicapped in a zoo, is that it? That's cruel.

JOE. Cruel?! You're calling me cruel!? I want to give him a contract. Give him his own show. Celebrate who he is and what he does. You want to change him. Beat it out of him. Who's cruel? *(Pause.)* Get him finished. Get him out of here.

MARIA *(handing him money)*. He has to get the five dollars from you. That was our agreement.

JOE *(strides over to MICHAEL)*. Here.

MICHAEL *(very nervous)*. I'm not finished. I've got to do the napkins and the forks and the/

JOE. I've seen your work. I know it's going to be beautiful. Here. Take it now.

MICHAEL. No. That's not right. I have to/

JOE *(gently but firmly)*. Here! It's a tip. Tips go on the table. Wherever. Right here. It's fine. No need to measure. *(Exits.)*

MARIA *(goes to table; MICHAEL is hyperventilating)*. It's all right. I'll hold your money till you're done. OK? Now, I've got to go feed the meter. I want you to be finished with the silver and starting on the glasses when I get back. *(MICHAEL is panicked. MARIA exits.)*

MICHAEL *(calling after her)*. It's against the rules to feed the meters.

(ELIZABETH enters.)

ELIZABETH *(in a hurry)*. Have you got change? *(MICHAEL stares at her, mesmerized, in love.)* For the meter.

MICHAEL. It's against the rules to feed the meters.

ELIZABETH. I just parked. I'm not feeding.

MICHAEL. You need quarters.

ELIZABETH. Yeah.

MICHAEL. Four quarters.

ELIZABETH. That'd be great, except I gotta break a five.

MICHAEL. I'm gonna get five dollars.

ELIZABETH. Uh...yuh.

MICHAEL. I'll get some change and then I'll give you some.

ELIZABETH. Uh, that'd be great.

MICHAEL. You're really beautiful.

ELIZABETH. Un-hunh, thank you. *(Pause.)* Were you going to get me some change?

MICHAEL. Yeah, sure, but first I have to finish setting this table.

ELIZABETH. Fine, so I should... I'll just wait by the cash register. OK?

MICHAEL. OK.

(ELIZABETH retreats to cash register. MICHAEL stares at her, she stares back, dumbfounded and feeling foolish. MARIA reenters.)

MARIA. Michael!

MICHAEL. She's beautiful.

MARIA. Michael, is this appropriate behavior?

MICHAEL. She's/

MARIA. Yes she is. She's a very attractive young lady. But I think you're making her a little uncomfortable. Excuse me, what's your name?

ELIZABETH. Elizabeth.

MARIA. Elizabeth, would you mind telling Michael what you're feeling right now?

ELIZABETH. He doesn't really work here, does he?

MARIA. Elizabeth, it would be very helpful if you could/

ELIZABETH. Whoa!

(ELIZABETH exits. MARIA frowns at MICHAEL. LYDIA enters.)

LYDIA. I have to open the dining room now. *(Pause.)* He'll have to go.

MARIA. All right. Let's go, Michael.

MICHAEL. I haven't finished.

MARIA. No, you haven't.

MICHAEL. I want the five dollars.

MARIA. If we don't meet our deadlines, we don't get our five dollars.

MICHAEL. But/

MARIA. Come along, Michael.

MICHAEL. NO!

MARIA *(controlling herself)*. I'm on a meter, too, Michael. While it's running, I will stand here, for hours if necessary, talking like Snow White and waiting for some little malignant psycho to place another fork. But the meter has run out. Do you understand? The little red flag just popped up. SNOW WHITE IS DEAD AND YOU'RE OUTTA HERE!

(MARIA grabs MICHAEL by his clothing and hurls him toward the door. LYDIA watches this, then hurriedly sets the table. QUINNE, SARAH, BETH and KATHERINE come in, place their coats on the back of the chairs at the two downstage tables and go to the buffet. ANNE and NICK enter in jogging attire, sit at MICHAEL's table and start taking off their shoes. LYDIA approaches their table.)

ANNE. I'll just have a Coke and some soda crackers.

NICK. Me, too. *(To ANNE.)* Will you look at that! Look at the size of this blister.

ANNE. Hey, me too. Same spot.

LYDIA. UMMM... we don't serve just Coke and soda crackers.

NICK. No kiddin'. Well just bring us a couple of menus. Yours is in the same spot, hunh?

LYDIA. We don't have a lunch menu. We have a buffet, $7.95 all you can eat, meatballs, salad/

ANNE. All-you-can-eat meatballs right after a 10K. I don't think so.

NICK. Oh, that's disgusting. Your blister's on the same side, hunh. Musta been that long traverse across the hill.

ANNE. Whatever. It's done now. Are you supposed to pop 'em?

NICK. Blisters? I always do. Hand me that fork, will you?

LYDIA. Don't touch that! You are the most disgusting pair that has ever walked in here, and you've had a lot of competition. *(She takes their shoes and throws them out the door.)* OUT!

(They hop one-footed out the door after their shoes. Lights up in the kitchen. MIRANDA is arranging crudités on a platter. ELI enters spraying the counter with one hand and wiping with the other. ELI sprays MIRANDA's tray of veggies. During the following, QUINNE, SARAH, BETH and KATHERINE return from the buffet with their plates and sit down.)

MIRANDA. Whoa! What's the matter with you?!

(ELI looks up.)

You ruined a whole plate of veggies.

(ELI holds up the spray bottle questioningly.)

Yeah!

ELI. So rinse 'em off. *(Goes back to cleaning.)*

MIRANDA. Rinse 'em off? Rinse 'em off. Are you nuts!? That stuff's industrial strength.

(ELI picks up a carrot off MIRANDA's tray, "cleans" it off by running it in and out of his mouth, and proceeds to set it back down. She slaps it out of his hand and it goes across the floor.)

It's got ammonia. It can kill you.

(ELI stops, looks at MIRANDA, opens his mouth, sprays in it, licks his lips, goes back to work. CARLOS enters.)

CARLOS. You finished? *(Sees veggies plate.)* It's about time. Last guy we had on this was faster than you, and I fired him for slow. Watch yourself. *(Takes the plate.)* Make the dip, both kinds.

MIRANDA. Uh... *(Trying to take plate back.)* Carlos. Uh, Eli just sprayed.

CARLOS. I don't wanna hear it. What!? You're gonna blame Eli 'cause you're a snail. Don't talk to me. Eli is the best of you. Youse should all be like Eli.

MIRANDA. But/

CARLOS *(pointing finger)*. Huh! *(MIRANDA shuts up. CARLOS exits with veggies.)*

(Back to dining room.)

QUINNE *(spears meatball from SARAH's plate and holds it up on her fork)*. What's this?

SARAH. Uh... my dinner? *(Pause, then apologetically.)* It was just a guess.

QUINNE. It's a meatball.

SARAH. Really?! You know, I was going to guess that but a little voice told/ me that no matter—

QUINNE. Do you have any idea what's in this so-called meatball?

SARAH. Well, there, uh, you see, once again, I think I know the answer but I'm sure I don't know *the* answer. *(Pause.)* Meat?

QUINNE. D-E-S.

SARAH. Uh, yeah, I was going to mention/ that

QUINNE. Di Ethyl Stilbesterol.

SARAH. All o' that? It's so small!

QUINNE. It causes birth defects.

SARAH. I was born fourteen years/ ago.

QUINNE. I'm not/ joking.

SARAH. And I'm not/ pregnant.

QUINNE. This is very, very/ serious.

SARAH. And DES was banned ten years ago.

QUINNE. What?

SARAH. It's banned, off the market, they don't use it anymore.

QUINNE. You think just because it's banned they don't use it anymore.

SARAH. No, I think you're still holding my dinner on the end of your fork.

(JOE enters in a trench coat with his back to them. He flashes open the coat and whirls around.)

JOE *(to QUINNE)*. You wanna buy a watch? *(Stunned silence. There are watches pinned all over the insides of his coat.)* I got Timex, Rolex, Elgin, Seiko, Hamilton *(with British affectation),* Helbrose, I got men's, I got ladies', I got digital, I got ana ... ana ... uh, whatchacallit, you know, with the hands going around. I got snooze alarms, built-in beepers, I got Mickey Mouse, I got Goofy, Spiderman, I got spandex, alligator, snake skin, I got religious, I got pornographic, whaddayalike? *(More silence.)* Am I confusing you? *(Silence.)* I'll take that as a "Yes." I'll start over. *(Mockingly slow.)* I got Swiss, Japanese, American, I got digital, analog, yeah, that's it, analog/ I got—

SARAH. Uh, waiter!?

JOE. Oh, excuse me. Am I bothering you?

QUINNE. We're not interested.

JOE. Oh, now you're not interested. Why didn't you say so? Why did you have to lead me on like that?

SARAH. We were *never* interested.

JOE. You were never interested. And you couldn't say so. Like I got oceans of time to spend doing my spiel for people who aren't even in the market. You got a lot of nerve. *(Sees LYDIA coming and moves away quickly and starts selling at another table.)*

LYDIA. Yes.

QUINNE. That man is bothering the customers, um, not to mention probably selling stolen goods.

LYDIA. Oh, that's just Joe.

QUINNE. Joe?

JOE *(at another table).* You wanna buy a watch?

LYDIA. Yeah. He's the owner. He thinks it's funny. A lot of the customers get off on it. That, and the meatballs. It keeps us in business.

JOE. I got Timex, Rolex, Elgin, Seiko, Hamilton *(with British affectation)*, Helbrose, I got men's, I got ladies', I got digital, I/

KATHERINE. I want the Minnie Mouse.

JOE. The Minnie Mouse?! You want the Minnie Mouse? You can't afford it. *(Starts to walk away, turns back.)* OK, what'll you give me.

(KATHERINE holds up a piece of avocado on her fork.)

   A piece of avocado?! Are you nuts?

BETH. I want the Minnie Mouse.

JOE. Oh you want the Minnie Mouse. You'll have to do better/ than your cheap friend here.

BETH. I'll give you a meatball.

JOE *(looks thunderstruck).* SOLD! *(He grabs the watch, rips it off his coat, hands it to BETH, seizes a meatball off of her plate, pops it in his mouth, chews, stops, pulls out the beard.)* Carlos!!!

(CARLOS runs in. JOE is holding up the disgusting wad of hair with two fingers.)

   Who made the meatballs?

CARLOS. Uh, Alalalalexandra!

JOE. ALEXANDRA!

(JOE charges off to the kitchen followed by CARLOS. JASON and KAREN enter from the buffet area with full plates and sit at MICHAEL's table.)

JASON *(sliding his spoon around on the tablecloth)*. WOW!

KAREN *(looking up)*. Wow?

JASON. Look how my spoon slides on this tablecloth.

KAREN. You're pushing it.

JASON. No, no, no no no. You don't understand. This... *(pushing chair back and focusing intently on the whole table)* this is it!

KAREN. Whatever you're about to do, don't. *(Pause.)* People are staring.

(JASON is reaching out to grip the tablecloth.)

Stop it!

JASON. This is the kind of tablecloth they use when they, you know, when they do that thing where they whip it away and leave all the dishes like totally undisturbed.

KAREN. Don't you dare. That takes years of practice and special trick dishes. Jason, listen to me.

JASON. No no! It's all in the cloth. This cloth. I just know. Didn't that ever happen to you, you know, all of a sudden you know something, and... and... and you weren't even thinking about it, like... like being touched by God or... or your fairy godmother or something? *(He stands, gripping the cloth.)*

KAREN. Sit down!

JASON. I'm sorry, Karen. I know you can't understand. You've never had an inspired moment in your life. But I want you to know that it hurts me that you can't believe in mine. Your lack of faith has always been so hard for me, striving to continue believing in myself when my best friend/

(All the kitchen staff create an audience for JASON.)

KATHERINE. I believe in you.

BETH. Me, too.

QUINNE. Go for it.

SARAH. Yeah, do it.

KAREN. Oh, no. Every time. Every time we go somewhere public you gotta pull some stunt. I'm not paying
for/

JASON. Ye of little faith. They believe.

KAREN. No, they just wanna see you make an ass of
yourself.

JASON. Noooo. They can see what you can't see. The
glow of divine inspiration. I'm gonna do it.

ALL OTHERS *(ad-lib)*. Go for it. We believe. Do it. *(Etc.)*

*(KAREN quickly rescues her plate, glass, fork and turns
away eating. JASON gets set, whips the tablecloth away
and makes a terrible mess.)*

BLACKOUT

BENEDICTION
by Steven Sater

CHARACTERS

MICAH: A young boy. Blind. By turns, introspective and feisty.

HODÉ: A middle-age black woman. Powerful. Magical. Fun-loving. Micah's imaginary friend.

JUDITH: A proper young girl. Micah's sister.

TIME: The present, late afternoon.
PLACE: Micah's room.

AT RISE: *MICAH sits by himself in a chair so big that his feet don't reach the floor. To the side of the chair, there's a great stack of colored cubes large enough to climb on. He rolls a white cane between his hands. Thinking. Silence, a moment. Then HODÉ emerges from deep within the earth, robed, and crowned, in seven kinds of precious jewels.*

MICAH. Hodé.
HODÉ. Yes, oh Most High and Excellent Master of the Universe.
MICAH. C'mon! Let's go!

(MICAH rises, hands HODÉ his stick, then climbs onto the cubes as if onto a jungle gym. He climbs like a monkey—avidly, having the time of his life. HODÉ sets the stick aside and follows after MICAH, scurrying along with him.)

MICAH. You know what we oughta do? Make a We-Hate-Older-Sisters Club.

HODÉ. You said it. 'Specially a We-Hate-Older-Sister-Judith Club.

MICAH. Yeah! We should, like, nuke her face off.

HODÉ. First her face, then her arms.

MICAH. Then we'll blast her legs off.

HODÉ. And bury 'em out in the yard.

MICAH. Or feed 'em to Ranger.

HODÉ. Cool!

MICAH. Make *her* do that book report.

HODÉ. Serves her right.

MICAH. I just hate her!

HODÉ. Hate her!

MICAH. Hate ... Her!

HODÉ. More than Robin Joiner?

MICAH. More than even Pattie Gooch Baker!

HODÉ. We should blow her up.

MICAH. Blow *her* up? We're gonna, like, blow up the whole butthead neighborhood.

HODÉ. The whole place?

MICAH. Yeah.

HODÉ *(excited)*. Cool! *(A beat.)*

MICAH. You got the bombs?

HODÉ. Sure I got the bombs.

MICAH. The right kind?

HODÉ. Duh.

MICAH. Excellent! *(Top secret.)* First, we're gonna start with the Nahems.

HODÉ *(a fellow conspirator)*. We'll pitch a big, big bomb right in their basement!

MICAH. Blow 'em right up!

HODÉ. All right!

MICAH. They're so dumb!

HODÉ. Such Doodyheads!

MICAH *(mocking the Nahems)*. "Can I help you, Micah?"

HODÉ *(joining in)*. "Let me help you, Micah."

MICAH. "Watch out for the curb, there, Micah."

HODÉ *(calling at the Nahems)*. Doodooheads!

MICAH. We'll cut out their eyes.

HODÉ. And dry 'em like raisins.

MICAH. We'll blow their stupid heads off!

HODÉ. Cool!

MICAH *(holds out his sword, a pledge)*. Best friends?

HODÉ *(laying her hand on the sword, taking the pledge)*. Best friends.

MICAH. Best. No matter what.

HODÉ. No matter what.

MICAH. To the death.

HODÉ. To the death.

MICAH. Got your sword?

HODÉ. Got it!

(MICAH and HODÉ stand, sword arms reared in triumph, at the top of the stack of cubes.)

JUDITH *(calling from off)*. Micah?

(MICAH suddenly falls silent. Terribly withdrawn. JUDITH again:)

Micah?

HODÉ. That butthead. Always bugging us.
JUDITH *(from off)*. Micah!

(MICAH retreats, resignedly climbing down from the stack of cubes, making his way back to his chair, and sinking into it. HODÉ follows, and hands MICAH his stick. JUDITH enters.)

JUDITH. So, there you are.
HODÉ *(sarcastic)*. So, there *you* are!
   (JUDITH cannot hear HODÉ, but MICAH smiles.)
JUDITH. What?
HODÉ *(imitating JUDITH)*. "What?"
JUDITH *(to MICAH)*. I heard you, you know.
HODÉ. You big dope!
JUDITH. Who were you talking to? *(No response.)* Your Hodé?
MICAH. No.
JUDITH *(teasing; singsong)*. Micah's talking to Hodé!
MICAH. I was not.
JUDITH. Were too.
MICAH. Was *not*.
JUDITH. Were too. Were too. Were too. So there. *(No response.)* Mom says it's time for dinner. *(No response.)* Micah?
MICAH. Okay.
   (JUDITH goes. A moment, then:)
   We're gonna megablast her stupid face off.
HODÉ. Lips and tongue and stupid, stupid face off!
MICAH. We're gonna neutro-neutralize her stupid tongue.
HODÉ. Cool! *(A beat.)*
MICAH. So... you wanna come to dinner?

HODÉ. You think your mom'll let me?
MICAH. I guess not. *(A beat.)* Well, dinner's stupid, anyway.
HODÉ. Real stupid. With their Brussels sprouts.
MICAH. Just stupid.
HODÉ *(calling off)*. Stupids!
MICAH. With their stupid pot of stupid gravy.
JUDITH *(from off)*. Micah! *(A beat.)*
MICAH. I gotta go.
HODÉ. Right. *(HODÉ descends deep into the earth.)*
JUDITH *(from off)*. Micah? *(No response.)* Micah, dinner!

(A moment, then MICAH rises, crosses toward the door of his room, tapping his way with his cane, as the lights fade.)

BLACKOUT

PREPARING THE MONOLOGUE

During a monologue, a private window opens into the soul of your character. Secret thoughts and yearnings of all shapes and dimensions, as well as dark and loving memories, are shared with other characters and/or the audience. For a few moments, the audience is given a glimpse of the private life your character generally keeps hidden beneath the surface. As an actor, you must discover what your character hopes to gain by revealing guarded information. The answer can never be "Because the playwright wrote it." The following tips and suggestions are intended to help prepare your monologue.

• Whenever possible, read the entire script. A monologue is a strategy your character is employing to secure an objective. Discover how your monologue fits into the fabric of the script as a whole, affording you the opportunity to texture your performance with shades of subtlety and meaning. However, since many monologues these days are being written especially for auditions, you are required to make your choices based on a close reading of the text only.

• Of paramount importance is to discover what the monologue is revealing about the character. Remember, the significance of the monologue rests in its ability to help the character achieve a particular goal. Is the monologue a justification of an action your character took against a friend or a parent? Is your character trying to rationalize behavior? Or is your character trying to summon up courage to confront an accuser or someone over whom your character has little clout or influence? Or is the monologue an attempt to come to a truthful understanding of why the character behaves(d) in a certain way? Or to come to a better understanding of why someone else behaves(d) in a certain fashion. Lastly, it is important to discover if the character is actually aware of the significance of the revelation(s). It may only be the audience or another character on stage that fully realizes the importance of the monologue when viewed against the full tapestry of the play or the scene.

• Divide the monologue into workable units. Actors sometimes launch into monologues in the belief that they have to plow through to the other side in as short a period of time as possible. But monologues are comprised of ideas and images. Listen to people when they tell you their stories of a failed relationship, or the arrival of a hated cousin, or the talk they finally had with the chemistry teacher about bad grades. There are usually some pauses while the person is thinking of the next word to say that will better communicate his or her feelings. Don't be afraid of silence. Silence is your ally as long as the material that follows the silence has been worth waiting for.

• Remember, stage dialogue is life-like in its sounds and rhythms but is far more compressed and detailed than real life. You may ramble at a coffee shop for two hours with three of your friends, but the same real-life dialogue would be tedious and repetitive if spoken on the stage. Stage language is heightened, choreographed to create an effect and lead the actor down the road to the heart of the character.

• Look for the operative words in each sentence, those words that seem to energize your character's attitude at any moment. Most often, these operative words will be verbs. Give those words special value and emphasis in your performance. Verbs such as grip, render, prove, unleash, promise, manage, throng, stack, squeeze and so on will allow you to "work" the word. For example, create a line using two active verbs and then read it with a sense of anger, surprise, nonchalance and so on. Notice how each word is stressed differently depending on the point of view brought to the material. Now add a few adverbs to the line and read it with a sense of derision, apprehension or righteousness. Again, the meaning rests not in the words and lines solely, but in the attitude your character has toward the content of the lines.

• Never approach a monologue as if it is a story about the past. It may deal with actions that occurred in the past, but the monologue must be provoked by the present situation facing your character. It must be an attempt to progress the plot, clarify a present confusion or summon courage to take an action that will make a difference now, not twenty years ago.

• When you begin memorizing your monologue, break it down into thought blocks, those sentences which cluster together to support an important idea or realization. Become familiar with the progression of ideas and insights within the monologue. Next, begin learning the monologue as a series of ideas joined to achieve a specific effect on the listener, or to reach an emotional awareness on the part of the character. Avoid memorizing lines in a vacuum. Always find a substantial, motivated reason to say the next line you are working on. If you memorize lines only, without knowing what they are intended to provoke or achieve, you will find it difficult to remember them during the heat of rehearsal and performance when you should be concentrating your energies on achieving your character's objective.

• A final word of caution. Don't feel you have to be emotional during a monologue. Acting is intended to engage an audience. Crying or yelling or rending your heart out on the stage runs the risk of being melodramatic. Stay with the reality of every moment. Stay connected to the material and don't be so concerned with the effect. The audience is your best friend. It wants you to succeed, to be convincing. It wants you to show it how to view life in a way that will help them with their own lives. Choose strong and well-written material, comic or serious, and be as honest as you can be in probing into the character's private world. Keep your attention on the work at hand, moment to moment, and you will be in control of the material and respectful of it at the same time.

Good luck!

MONOLOGUES FOR MEN

RAISING MOM
by Mike Thomas

(JERRY is remembering the confrontation he had with his mother whom he caught shoplifting.)

Jerry

Mom used to give me these nice gifts to give to my teachers when I was in elementary school. Valentine's Day earrings, little things like that. But we never had a lot of money and the teachers would just look at me and smile but say "no thank you." I didn't want Mom to feel hurt or anything so I just threw them away after school and told her the teachers said they were pretty. As I got older I saw what was happening. I'd be coming around the end of the aisle at K-Mart and I'd see her putting something in her purse, a comb or some toothpaste or maybe a necklace.

I was fourteen when a guy in a blue coat just stepped right in front of us. Mom told me to wait in the parking lot. It got so late I didn't know if she was ever coming out of the store. Then she came out, got in the car and we drove away. I never said anything. We never shopped there again even though it was the closest place.

I used to play it over and over in my head how I'd ask her to please quit "taking things," or maybe I'd say "stealing stuff" instead. *(Pause.)* I was scared of losing her. What if she got arrested? But I never said nothing and she kept

193

taking stuff. Then last year I was walking out the front door to meet my friends at the bowling alley and Mom was watching reruns. "Be careful, Jerry, I love you," and I turned around and screamed at her, "I love you too... could you stop stealing stuff in the store!" Just like that. It just came out of me like I was barfing. She gave me this hard look like I was clear outta line. I thought she was going to deny it, but instead she said, "I didn't know it bothered you." And I said it did, it bothered me a lot, and tears just started coming out of my eyes.

I told her how it scared me that she might be taken away from me and we only had each other. But she was real calm. "Well," she said, "I only take things to give other people." But she promised me she wouldn't do it anymore and went back to watching her reruns.

I haven't seen her do it in a long time. But since that day, things have been different with me and my mom. In some ways I'm sorry I ever said anything. You're not supposed to have conversations like that with your mother.

THE FREAK MEISTER
by Ric Averill

(The Freak Meister stands dressed very uniquely in front of a group of teachers and peers. He/she is at an audition and hasn't prepared anything, so the director says, "Just tell us about yourself—anything—maybe, why you dress the way you do.")

NOTE: This piece can be performed by a woman under the title of The Mistress of Freaks.

Freak Meister

I am the Freak Meister. I haunt the halls. I am individual and cannot be defined. I wrote this monologue. I'm writing my entire life, in fact, and doing it so that no one will ever be able to figure me out.

I will be unique. I will be completely different. The one person about which nothing can be stereotyped. This is a challenge. There are so many uniforms of uniqueness. I leaned toward black garments until it became too Goth. I tried the button-down look, polyester, retro seventies, hippie sixties, even a brief return to the fifties.

The terrible thing is this. As I change my look, waves of people gravitate toward me—and they all look like me. So each look only lasts about five days until I realize myself to be one of the many conformists to nonconformity.

Maybe I'll become invisible. If I can't be seen, I'll haunt the halls and no one will know who I am, where I am, or what to expect of me.

I will be unique. Unseen. Alone.

Because I want to be appreciated. Noticed. Loved.

I am the Freak Meister. I haunt the halls.

ART CLASS
by Mike Thomas

(TEDDY has been sent to the school counselor by his art class teacher. TEDDY is sensitive and confused. Violence frightens him.)

Teddy

I didn't want to come to this school in the first place... I liked where I was, but Dad got transferred and I've been doing everything I'm supposed to, but some of the guys want to fight or call me names, look big to their friends. They knock my books out of my hands or throw snowballs at me. So I'm in Ms. Jenkins' art class and I'm making the wooden model thing she's wanting us to make, and Bobby Clancy comes over and starts calling me a "Mama's Boy" and laughing with his friends. And I'm ignoring him, you know? Just keeping my head down and working on that stupid wooden model, and he starts shoving me! And I look up and Ms. Jenkins ain't there. Where'd she go? She's not in the room.

"Look at the little fag playing with his little toy!" and I give him some kind of look—my Dad always says just look 'em right in the eyes and the bullies will back down—but Bobby Clancy just gives me the

(Hitting his chest, imitating Clancy's taunting style.)

"C'mon, punk" stuff, and I couldn't help laughing. He looked so stupid, like he was in a zoo and beating on his chest. That must have got to him 'cause he picked up the model glue and squirted it right in my face. The fumes burned my eyes and some of it got into my mouth, and he starts pointing at me and saying "Oooohhh, looks like he gave somebody a good time. Did you give someone a good time, you little faggot?" And then I just... uh... I grabbed his black jacket and wiped my mouth off on it, smeared glue all over it. So he hits me in the chest and yells something about that being a new coat and I was going to pay for it, and he's raising his arm to hit me and I just picked up my American History book and swung it with both hands. Hit him right in his face, bloodied his nose. He fell backwards and hit his head on the floor. I didn't mean for it to happen, but I think he's hurt.

Ms. Jenkins... she appeared out of nowhere and told me to come see you. So I backed out the door and here I am. I can't stop shaking. I'm in trouble, aren't I? But everybody keeps pushing at me. That ain't fair, right? God, I hate this school. Why'd Ms. Jenkins have to leave the room?

TALKING IN THE NIGHT
by Caridad Svich

*(TRUCO, a young man, sells driftwood on a dead-end
island devastated by war, and dreams of a better life.)*

Truco

I remember I used to sit up at night, listen to the radio,
back when we were still getting it,
late at night when most people had gone to bed,
and I'd get this station,
and I swear I didn't know where it was coming from,
I only knew that wherever it was
was someplace I had to be.
Cause you'd hear these voices—
people talking,
calling in for a song, telling their stories,
and they sounded happy.
Like the place they were living
freed them of responsibility,
like they could do anything they wanted
long as they took care
not to run someone else down while they were doing it.
Bold, well-fed voices
that spoke of good living and plenty,
that had none of this gasping I'd come to expect,
that little struggle in the breath,
I was so used to hearing in the folks
who made their life round here.

Voices that come from a place where just about anybody
could get themselves a piece of land,
where a little hard work could make you
a whole lot of money,
and a certain kind of peace was guaranteed at day's end.
It was the voices,
more than the songs
(although they too had a feeling of possibility)
that made me listen in the long hours of night,
listen, and dream.

DAD LEFT ON SOME FAST REINDEER
by *Mike Thomas*

(TONY is 18 going on 35. He is recalling the night his dad left his family.)

Tony

It's Christmas, OK? It's raining and it's Christmas Eve. And we're sitting around, opening gifts, drinking soda. Me, Mom, Dad and my little brother Matt. And Dad says he's out of cigarettes and he's gonna run down to the store real quick before Santa drops by. *(Pause.)* And he never comes back. Mom didn't seem too surprised. After about two hours, Mom just sort of...started crying, rocking back and forth, crying. I hugged her tight and said I was going to bed, but I just sat in the hall. My little brother Matt asked where Daddy was and my mom told him "Daddy left on some fast reindeer tonight." And Matt asked if he was going to come back, and Mom started singing Christmas carols. And the room glowed all weird with the Christmas tree lights blinking against the rain.

I wanted to tell her that we'd all be fine without the bastard but I couldn't speak to my mom like that, so the next morning I broke every ashtray in the house. I broke thick, green glass ones, I broke white plastic ones. I even broke the ugly purple one I gave him on Father's Day when I was ten—hit 'em all with Dad's sledgehammer. *(Pause.)* I went through every closet and Dad's desk drawers. I broke every single ashtray in the house. I thought that would make my mom stop crying, but she got mad at all the glass and crap in the driveway and made me clean it up. I never could talk to her right.

I don't know who I am sometimes. You get a lot from your old man, that's what I bet. I can see it with other guys and their dads. But I know one thing. I hate Christmas.

LOVING BESS
by Jett Parsley

(TIB is 20. He is talking about Bess, the girl he loves.)

Tib

I was six, walkin' to school, takin' a shortcut by the creek. First day of school. First time I ever saw her. She wasn't at school. She was in the creek. Hoppin' over the stones, splashin' hard, on purpose, soakin' herself. Knowin' she had school, knowin' she couldn't go in there wet. You got to love a person like that. Don't you? She don't kiss like no one I ever kissed. She don't seem to be there. Her mind ain't on the task, thinkin' 'bout other things. You'd think that'd make a guy mad. I 'spose it does. Makes you so mad you start kissin' her more. You get determined to find her. You decide somehow, some way, *you* are goin' to be the one to get her mind where her lips are. *You* are goin' to be the one to make her stop splashin' and stay dry. *You*. Then she walks out. She says, "Enough, Tib Johnson, I got things to do without you." And she leaves you standin' in the creek, your pants wet, your toes numb in the cold water, wishin', wishin' you could jump, make a splash, splatter the cold water over her back as she moves away so she'd turn around and look at you—one more time—even if she only keeps walkin'. *You* gotta be the one to make her turn around. You gotta be the one. *You.*

X-MAN
by Silvia Gonzalez S.

(X is a gang member with still-fine baby-face features and a thin body. He is shirtless, wears baggy pants with his underwear showing at the top. He stares at a baby in a stroller.)

X *(proudly)*

I am a man. Look at me, lil' one. I am a man. You've proved it to me. You are like this gun.

(He pulls out a gun from his pocket.)

See, this gun has proved to me that I am a man, too. *This* and *you* prove that I am someone to be admired. I'm real tough shit. I'm an incredible human being. I'm so great I can hardly hold my head up. Hey, can you see how big my head is, lil' one? Can you? I have a big head because I know I am a man. I'm soooo tough, everyone better respect me. First a gun, and then a baby. A gun, and then a baby.

(His mood changes.)

I'm full of shit. You don't like this gun, do you? I didn't at first, but then it got to be very important. Then you come along and I see something else.

(He puts the gun into his pants.)

If only I had kept it in my pants you wouldn't be here. Hell, I didn't even like her. One of those things. I'm too young to be a father! Damn. What did I go and do? I must've been high when it happened because I don't even

204

remember it. I jacked up my life. Damn, what did I go and do that to myself for?

(He takes out the gun and looks at the baby. He points the gun at the stroller. He stands there for a long while and then melts.)

What am I doing? Shit!

(He drops the gun in the trash. He picks up the baby.)

I'm going to have to teach you things I've learned on the way. Some stuff that came to me the hard way. You saw my piece, huh? It's my *ex*-piece starting today. That piece doesn't make anyone into a man. And you know something, even *making you* doesn't make a man. It's teaching you to respect yourself without anyone's approval—that's what makes you into a man. If I teach that to you real good, then you won't end up like me. You see, I thought I would be dead before I ever saw fatherhood, but then you went and came into my life.

(Smiling.)

What a thing to do to me, huh. You went and changed my life. What a thing to do to your dad, huh. You like to mess people up, huh. Yeah, you do. You are just like me.

(Realizes.)

Just like me? Hell no.

(He cradles the baby with more tenderness. His face turns to innocence.)

You know something, together we got to prove to the world that a *real* man doesn't have to prove it. What do you say we only prove it to each other? I teach you to be good to yourself and not need to impress anyone, and you hang out with me and remind me that *I'm your dad* and don't gotta get respect from anyone, but you. Deal?

PLAYGROUND
by Ric Averill

(BRANDON is seated, discouraged, talking to his girl-friend, not a girlfriend, but a girl friend. He is being philosophical about an incident that has him in trouble.)

Brandon

I punched a kid today. When I was walking past the grade school playground. I know it's not logical. The kid didn't do anything except say, "What are you looking at?"

That made me mad. I was looking at these kids as they played. Just like we used to play. They didn't care about anything. They didn't care about society, grades, acne, getting a date, AIDS, drugs, parents, or anything that I can't get off my mind.

They were just playing. And it seemed indecent to me. I mean, I know that I'd rather have jumped in amongst them and played tag or steal the bacon or red rover or something. I'd love to lose myself in play so that when my mother calls me home, I'm startled that there's a reality besides the play we're doing.

But it's not that way anymore. I have to worry. It's my job. Go to school and study too hard, impress people and be grown up.

I'm not even a bully. I baby-sit on weekends. I've never done a violent thing in my whole life, except the one time Tommy Meyers and I tied firecrackers to the cat's tail— but that was a long time ago and I had nightmares about it for weeks.

I think I'll have nightmares again. This kid that I punched in the stomach looked up so wounded. I don't think I really hurt him. I know I didn't send him to the emergency room or anything, it's just...he looked so free. And I'm so ...not.

When he looked at me with that big "why?" on his face, it was like...like looking in a mirror. It should have made me feel bad, but I just wanted to hit him again.

His mom called mine. I'm going to have to wash their cars or something. I don't really mind. I just hope the kid isn't around. Not that I can't control myself. I'm not going to do it again. But I just don't want the reminder. Why do we have to grow up when it'd be so much easier to grow down?

THE LONG WAY HOME
by Ted Sod

Sam

The first thing they do to you is put you on Valium—
they're afraid once you come down you'll get the shakes.
They ask you a ton of questions about your drug habit.
What do you take and how much? When did you start
usin'? Alone or with people? Where you got it from. You
walk down the hallways and everybody checks you out—
they stare at you 'cause they know you're new—they've
all been there themselves. I had no clothes, no comb,
nothin' personal. I didn't look at anybody, because I knew
I'd either get into a fight or start throwin' stuff. I just bit
my nails and my lips. I didn't see my father for five
days—they don't want any family contact. They hand you
a stack a books—the big book, pamphlets on AA, Narcot-
ics Anonymous. They don't let you watch TV, so you
don't have any choice. You can stare at the walls or read. I
stared at the walls, cried, threw furniture around and finally decided to read. Somewhere in the second week I
gave in to it. I called my father and told him to bring me
some clothes. My father asked me if I was mad at him. I
told him I was mad at him because he never hugged me. I
told him I was mad at him because we never talked. I told
him I was mad because he lied to Mom about his girl-
friends. I told him I know he was disappointed in me because he always wanted me to be tough and I'm not tough.
I'm weak. He said I'm not weak—he said it takes guts to

208

say what I just said to him. He said if I was weak, I'd a never been able to make it through two weeks of treatment. He said he was proud of me. That made me laugh. I had to get hooked on drugs and go into rehab for him to tell me that I finally did something right.

MONOLOGUES FOR WOMEN

THE RIGHT BOX
by *Eleanor Harder*

(A school hallway. TINA (or TOM), a high school student, stomps in angrily, carrying a paper and pen, stops, and addresses audience.)

Tina

I'm really steamed! I have to fill out this dumb form, and it's got these little boxes that say "Caucasian," "Black," "Asian," "Native American," "South Pacific," and stuff, and I'm supposed to check which one I am. Why do they have to know *what* I am? I'm *me*, that's what I am! And I told the lady that, and she gives me this bored look and says, *(imitating)* "Just check the right box and bring it back to me!" The right box? I don't fit in any of them.

(Grins.)

I have a friend who told them she was "Blaxican," and she didn't see any box for that. Well, I could say that, too. Blaxican, I mean, 'cuz I've got some black on my dad's side and Mexican on my mom's. But my dad's great-grandfather was Native American, and my mom's grandmother was Irish! So—what am I? I don't see any box here for me.

(Shakes her head.)

We've got this big ol' dog. Got him out of the pound when he was just a puppy. He's two now, and nobody can figure out what he is. Well, he's a mix, we know that. But a mix of what is a real mystery. He's got a lot of fur that I guess you'd call multicolored, and his tail can't decide to

curl up or down, and his eyes are kind of yellowish. I'm
making him sound terrible. But he's really a great-looking
dog. And when we took him to the vet's for his shots, the
vet said so, too. He said he could have some German
shepherd and collie, maybe some chow, even a little coy-
ote in him, he wasn't sure, but he was certainly a splendid-
looking dog. That's just what he said—a splendid-looking
dog. I know they call dogs that aren't purebreds "mutts."
So, *(shrugs)* guess ours is a mutt. A splendid-looking one.

(Thinks.)

Then maybe people like me are mutts, too? I don't think I
like the sound of that. Mutts. Somewhere I read that mutts
are stronger than purebreds, and they live longer, too. I
don't know if that works for human mutts, but I hope so.
'Course, when I think of the people I know, or have heard
about, most of them are mutts, too. Well, like, most everybody's a mix of something. So what does that mean?
We're *all* stronger, and we'll *all* live longer? I don't know.

(Looks at paper.)

Maybe I'll just write down "mutt" on this. I can just see
that lady's face when I hand it in.

(Grins.)

Or maybe I'll make up a name just for me, like—

(Thinks.)

Hmm—Native American, Irish, Black and—Nate-Am-Iri-
Blaxicana. Nate-Am-Iri-Blaxicana.

(Repeats in rhythm.)

Nate-Am-Iri-Blaxicana! Yeah! Sounds good! A lot better
than mutt.

(Grins as she marks paper.)

There. Now *that's* the *right* box!

(Exits triumphantly.)

I'M GONNA WANNA GOTA COLLEGE
by John O'Brien

Student

I want to go to college. Notice I said "want to go to." That's not what my mother says. She says "wanna gota." "Why do you wanna gota college for?" she says. After I stop wincing, I say, "Not 'wanna gota,' Mother. It's 'want to go to.' " "Is you correcting me?" she says. "Of course I'm correcting you," I say. "If one makes a mistake, one should be corrected." "One who?" she says. "It's just a way of speaking, Mother. 'One' means you." "One, two, buckle my shoe," she says. I'd tell her that was a non sequitur, but what's the use? "In proper English, Mother," I say, " 'one' refers to someone." "I ain't someone," she says. "Everybody is someone," I say. "I'm your mudda," she says. "I know you're my mother, Mother," I say. "I'm glad to hear that," she says. "I wasn't sure you did."

That's the way our conversations begin. They go downhill from there. I don't mean to pick on my mother. I just don't understand why she says things wrong two minutes after I tell her what's right. "Lay down," she says to the dog, no matter how many times I tell her it should be, "Lie down." "What difference does it make?" she says. "He laid down, didn't he?" " 'Lay down,' Mother." "Why should I lay down?" she says, "I just got up. Besides, the dog don't care how we talk." "The dog doesn't care, but I do. I want to talk right because someday I want to talk to people about something other than shopping malls, earrings, and bingo." "You know your trouble?" she says. "You think you're better than your family." My family is my three sisters and four brothers. I'm the youngest. None of the seven has been to college. Three of the seven dropped out of high school. The man who calls himself my father works two jobs plus another one on weekends. I haven't seen him in a fortnight. He drove past me as I was coming out of the library. I know it was him because he waved to me. At least I think he waved. Maybe he was just scratching his head, wondering who I was.

"You wanna talk like rich people," my mother says. " 'Want to,' Mother, not 'wanna,' and rich isn't the point. I want to talk as well-educated people talk. Is that a crime?" "Like them snobs that lives in Cedar Grove." " 'Those' snobs, Mother, and they're not all snobs." "The ones I know is." " 'Are,' Mother, 'are.' " "You gotta sore throat?" she says, pretending she thinks I said 'ahh.' "You don't look sick." "I'm sick of people who want to remain ignorant," I say. That does it. "Now she's calling me ignorant," she says, turning to talk to the dog. "There's no shame in being ignorant, Mother. The only shame is in remaining ignorant." I don't tell her that I read that somewhere on a bumper sticker. "Ignorant means not knowing," I say. "I want to know." "Waddya wanna know?" "I want to know what's out there." She was waiting for that one. "Turn on TV," she says, "They'll tell you the weather every half hour."

I don't say that conversation with my mother was typical, but it wasn't untypical, either. Actually, the only adult I can really talk to works at the school. It's neither a teacher

nor a guidance counselor. Who it is may surprise you, especially if you live in one of the Cedar Groves of America. It's a custodian, a lady custodian. Her name is Marie.
The kids call her the "lady." They don't mean it as a put-
down. They call the teachers—the ones they don't know—
the "ladies" and the "guys." On the first day of school
last year, I asked my friend Darlene: "Who's your homeroom teacher?" "Some lady," she said. "Who do you
have for English?" I asked. "Some guy," she said. Back
to Marie, the custodian. One reason I like her is she has a
sense of humor. She doesn't take herself too seriously, or,
as my mother would say, "She don't take herself too serious." My mother thinks girls—she calls all females, including my grandmother, girls—shouldn't be custodians.
She thinks it's not nice. My mother has more hang-ups
than a cloakroom.

I like to get to school early to talk to Marie, while she
vacuums the rug in my homeroom. I'd like to meet the
rocket scientist who installed wall-to-wall carpeting in a
classroom. It's caked with gum and candy, and who knows
what else? Marie says: "Young people need to express
themselves." She doesn't smile when she says it, until I
do, and then she does. When I tell her about my troubles
at home, she says: "Why don't you meet your mother
halfway?" "What should I do," I say, "talk bad English
every other sentence?" "You know that's not what I
mean," she says. "Do you agree with my mother?" I ask.
"I sympathize with her," she says. "After I graduate from
college," I say, "I'll have time for sympathy."

Marie stops vacuuming and looks at me. Whenever she does that, I have a strange feeling that I have two mothers. "Your mother can't stop you from going to college," she says. "It isn't against the law." "She can tell me she won't help me with the tuition," I say. "Apply for a scholarship." "She can make me pay rent for my room at home." "Work after school." "If I work after school, I won't have time to study." "Then go to college part-time." "That will take years." "But you'll be doing it. That's what counts, not how you do it, but doing it. If you want to do it, do it." Marie resumes vacuuming.

When I come home from school, I smile at my mother. "What is you up to?" she says. "Me's?" I say. "Nuttin'." "How come you looks so happy?" "I'm happy, Mother, because I seen the light." "It's about time," she says. "Cheat at school?" "No, I skipped lunch to study for a test." "Let's gota the mall and get a coupla roast beef sangwiches, boat wid." For a moment, I'm stumped, and she knows it. "Boat wid mayonnaise," she says. "Don't you know nuttin'?" I go to my mother and hug her. She is suspicious. "What brang that on?" she says. "We're just a coupla boat wids, Mother, boat wid our own problems." "Sometimes," she says, "I wonder why I brang you up." "I'm glad you did," I say, and we're off to the mall.

AFTER THE WAKE
by Carida Svich

*(SIMONE, a young woman, who has just lost her hus-
band in an unnamed war, is left alone by her commu-
nity in a Louisiana bayou. She is seated, surrounded by
buckets of Kentucky Fried Chicken.)*

Simone

Chicken.
Buckets and buckets of fried chicken all over.
Twelve, sixteen, twenty-four piece...
Everybody brought one. One kind or another.
Caroline, Selah, Mrs. Hawkins...
They all came in with their chicken.
They all came in.
With their mouths open. Gristle stuck between their teeth.
Their faces smeared with grease, and perfume, and liquor.
They all came in.
Came in and flapped their arms. Calling out to God
and Jeremiah and all the powers in the universe.
They all came in with their chicken.
Came in to push their thigh meat in my face.
Push it in my face to make me feel better.
I thought I'd puke.
I thought, "One more bucket, I'm gonna
get down on my knees
and puke right next to the coffin."
I don't like fried chicken. He sure as hell didn't.

Why'd they bring it, then? Cause that's what you do?
That's what you do when somebody passes on?
Y'know, just because people been doing something
a long time
don't mean you gotta KEEP ON doing it.
Ain't nobody said you gotta become a fool to tradition.
Why didn't they bring something else?
Sweet potato pie, ice water, hard whiskey...
I wouldn't have minded some hard whiskey.
But fried chicken?
It smells up the whole house.
Smells up the house real good.
Why, you can smell the stink of the fat for miles.
Clear up to the river, you can smell it.
Grease all over.
Goes straight through the buckets, stains the wood.
HELL to get grease out once it stains the wood.
Fingers get oily, sticky, hands reeking of chicken.
Grease swimming through you until NOTHING
can rid you of its reek.
Gotta get tar soap, wash it off, scrub your hands blood raw
to get rid of it.
And the thing is, who's gonna eat it?
Who is gonna eat the damn chicken anyway?
I can't eat it. And he's dead.
What good's it going to do him?
Peel off the skin and fat and throw the chicken bones
at him,
that's all I can do.,
Bury him with the chicken bones...
Dead. Just dead.

Some bullet ripped right through him
like he was dog-meat;
eyes all busted, bones sticking out of the flesh...
I didn't even recognize him.
If they didn't say it was Jamie, I wouldn't know
who it was, so little left of him that's really him...
He was my husband, Jamie was.
Damn war killed him off.
I don't even know where it was.
All I know, one day there was a rumor of war,
and the next, he was off to some little country
somewhere I couldn't even
find on a map. And then he was dead...
We weren't even married a month.
Made love in some car, got married.
And he just TAKES OFF.
BASTARD.
I can barely remember him now.
I'll see somebody, he'll look like him,
but he'll turn around and I realize
he don't look like Jamie at all.
Not even married a month.
And all I got are buckets of chicken
stinking up the house. That's all I got.
Fried chicken and a dead body.

SHOOTING STAR
by James Still

(JESS, a 15-year-old girl, talks to us as if she's talking to a best friend. The feeling is like someone who's reliving an important moment, sharing a great secret.)

Jess

I'm not kidding! I wipe the sweat from my face and squint up at the scoreboard. It reads:

Home 67 Visitors 67 / Time: Zero-Zero-Zero.

I step up to the free-throw line and stare up at my future: a glass backboard, an orange hoop, a white net. Two free throws. If I make either one—we'll beat Central Heights for the first time in five years.

The gym is vibrating from all the noise. Out of the corner of my eye I can see my mom mouthing the words, "Go Jess!" On the bench, Coach Olson is biting a hangnail and all of my friends are yelling, "Sink it!" It feels like the whole world is watching. The referee bounces the ball toward me...his nose kind of looks like a light bulb. I take a deep breath and squeeze the basketball with both hands, hoping nobody will see that I'm shaking. *(Beat.)* There's a tan line on my finger where I used to wear Rob's class ring. When I told Rob I wanted to play sports this year he smiled and said, "No problem, babe." Then when I told him I wanted to play BASKETBALL he said, "Big problem, babe." My high school doesn't have a girl's basketball team so it meant I'd be playing for the boy's team...for Rob's team. As soon as practice started and word got out —I was like a celebrity. Newspaper reporters started popping up at practice, hounding my friends, and calling my house. I was interviewed on the TV-9 evening news. My mom even got a call from *20/20* because they'd heard about some girl playing for the boys team. That would be me.

At the first game of the season, cheerleaders chanted, "Jess, Jess, she's our man, let's give her a great big hand!" The crowd had a good laugh—but we won and I had three rebounds and six points. Rob only had four points. After the game he asked for his ring back. That night at home, Mom made me a peanut butter and banana sandwich and said, "Rob Tyler's as shallow as a baby pool, anyway!" It made me laugh, but still...I felt rotten.

So there I am at the free-throw line. I square up, bend my knees, my elbows are in, I release the ball, my follow-through is...perfect. The ball is spinning through the air in slow motion...it hits the side of the rim, rolls around the basket once, twice, dips, balances...and falls out.

I missed it.

The crowd gets real quiet and then I hear my mom scream, "You can do it, Jess!" I have one more chance to make it and win the game.
    (JESS stares up at the goal.)
"Come on. Please let me make it."

(She squares up, bends her knees and shoots the ball. She watches it like it's in slow motion.)
The gym is so loud it feels like the ceiling is going to burst open and the basketball's going to land in the Big Dipper. But the ceiling doesn't move and the ball is coming down toward the basket and someone from the other team yells, "Air ball!" My heart stops. And then like a shooting star, the basketball falls through the hoop without touching the rim. Swish!

There's total silence for one-half of one-half of one-half of a second that seems to last nine thousand years. A blink. A breath. A heartbeat. And then the whole place just explodes into a party. My teammates lift me on their shoulders, Coach Olson is waving his chewed-up fingers in victory, and my mom is jumping up and down blowing kisses in my direction. The school band starts playing that old song, "I Am Woman" and everybody's giving me high-fives. I look up at the scoreboard and it reads:

Home 68 / Visitors 67

We won!

"Hey, Jess!" I turn around and Rob says, "Way to go." I just nod. I didn't know what to say. Over Rob's shoulder there's a little girl trying to dribble a basketball—and she's doing it all wrong. I go over to her just as she's about to give up in frustration. "You want to dribble with your fingertips," I tell her. "That's it. Keep your head up." The little girl listens. Rob's listening too. "Always keep your head up." The little girl gives me a high-five. Rob's smiling at me for the first time in weeks.

A SMOKE AND A LINE
by *Caridad Svich*

(MIRANDA, a young woman, tries to console Simone, a young grieving widow.)

Miranda

My grammy would take me fishing when I was little.
Yeah, she'd take me. I didn't know what was going on.
"Grammy, what's this? Grammy, what's that?"
"Hush, child," she'd say, "hush."
Swear don't know how she put up with me, but she did.
She'd just smile ... sit there ... fish.
She'd smoke, too.
Not cigarettes, but a big old cigar bout this thick.
You should've seen the smoke
she'd blow out of that thing.
Swirls and swirls of it. Like chimney smoke.
Used to make them herself, the cigars.
Grow the tobacco out back, roll the leaves up in the finest
paper,
suck on it 'til one end'd be completely wet
with her saliva and juice, and then she'd light up,
the raw tobacco just enveloping the air.
Oh, and she'd smile ... she'd smile the biggest grin.
Teeth turned black, she'd still smile.
I hated it. All of it. The cigars. Everything.
Felt like it was a punishment every time I had to go out
with her.

225

Grammy and her damn tobacco.
But after a while, I don't know how it occurred,
the smell of that tobacco became like heaven itself.
"When we going fishing, Grammy? When we going?"
"Patience, child," she'd say, "patience."
And she'd smile, gather her gear,
and take me down to the water.
The sun'd be coming up. You could see the rays just peering.
Flashes of light bouncing off the water blinding you
as you looked into the morning haze.
And she'd smile, lay out the tobacco,
and start rolling them cigars,
her hands moving sharp and quick
like one of those gunfighters on the TV,
all eyes and trigger fingers.
Rolling and lighting up. Smoking and casting a line.
It was all of a piece with Grammy.
I'd sit there, wallowing in the smell,
swear all angels had come down to pay us a visit.
Used to try to catch the rings of smoke with my mouth,
like some sort of weird human kind of fish.
I swear, it was the best part of going fishing.
In fact, for the longest time, that's what I thought fishing was:
just something you did to go smoking.

CAUGHT
by Ric Averill

(LOUISE, a teenage girl, is talking to a therapist. Her mother has arranged for them to have family counseling. LOUISE is reluctant but agrees to talk.)

Louise

I don't really know why I'm here. My mom says I need therapy, but that doesn't make sense to me. I didn't do anything wrong and I already know that. I think Mom just wants company 'cause she can't handle it.

All of her friends say it's my dad's fault. OK, I'm closer to Mom's friends than Dad's, but, then again, I don't see his friends anymore.

I know they both love me. I really do. Mom gets mad when I tell her that, of course. Dad doesn't. He just gets this kind of faraway look in his eyes and says, "We all make mistakes, Louise, baby. Some of us just get caught."

So I started following my mom a little more closely, and that's how I figured out about Steve. I was proud of her going on a date. I really was. We joked about maybe double-dating, but that would be sooo kinky. Anyway, I stayed up, like she used to for me before the divorce. I watched from the second-floor window as they drove up.

My dad never liked Steve.

"He's always had everything, never had to work for it," Dad said.

Anyway, I watched Steve and my mom in his car and they kissed—no, they made out. I could tell it wasn't the first time.

I don't know why I cried. I guess it's because "Steve always gets everything" and now he has my mom. I know my dad cheated, but I didn't see it. I guess the person who is most wrong is the person who gets caught.

I tell you this. I'm never getting caught. AND, I'm never getting married.

PUNK GIRLS
by *Elizabeth Wong*

(GREEN PUNK, 20s, is in "dangerous" clothing. Spray-paint can in hand.)

Green Punk

How can you be so calm? I'm in a crisis here! This is eating me up from the inside out! I'm stinking. And putrid from the rot of my own pathetic spiritual indifference. Explain it to me. Help me to understand. I'm lost. The universe is exploding. It's blowing up. It's a car bomb right to our very souls.

*(GREEN PUNK paints, "*NO HOPE,*" on the wall or floor.)*

I'm bubbling, gurgling in a death grip... And you talk about the goodness of the universe? The goodness of God? I'm talking about human suffering. I'm talking about the enormous amount of human pain arising from omnipotent design. Poverty, oppression, persecution, war, injustice, indignity, inequity. These are evils, manifestations of sin. Palpable, inescapable, undeniable. This is the dilemma of our age.

This is THE question. This is the root cause of helplessness, and hopelessness, and universal despondency, and rap music! Stop the Bahrainians from clitorectomies. Stop children from toiling for slave wages. Restore the Dalai Lama! Save Sri Lanka from genocide. Save Bosnia from genocide. Mass graves in Rwanda. Mass graves in Bosnia. Mass graves in Cambodia. The starving in Korea. The starving everywhere. Decaying families under secret graves. The hand of God, the artwork of God in man. One million dead in Rwanda. Two million refugees in Tanzania. And Burundi. Oh God, what about Burundi? Poor little Burundi. Where is Burundi? Where is God? And you wonder why G.H.B., Xtasy!! And the rain forest! Unspeakable acts of suffering by governments, by military minds, warring tribes, political factionalism! Tears of innocent war-torn children! Soaking the crust of the earth, right down to the grave...crystal, pot, speed, Drano, laughing gas? I need to pray.

(Softly, muttering.)

Microsoft, Merck, R.J. Reynolds, I.B.M., Microsoft, Sony, Hallmark, Microsoft, Proctor, Gamble, Microsoft...

(GREEN PUNK on her knees, mumbling fervent prayer.)

FRECKLE FAITH
by Nancy Hanna

(EDIE is a teenager from Caddo Lake, Texas. She talks to her doll, combing its hair with her fingers—the doll can be pantomimed. In bold: The voice of the doll.)

Edie

You're beautiful. **"Oh stop."** No, no, you are. The day Mama brought you home from town, she said, "Edie, here's your new best friend. I want you to meet Miss Sally Mae Fontune." At least that's how Aunt June remembers it. **"Edie I heard this all before."**

(She ignores the voice of the doll.)

"Named after the Fon-tune Blue Hotel in Miami, Florida. You and her are going to be best friends, an' paint your fingernails, an' go to Hot Springs together, an' order double-fudge sundaes at the fancy hotel." **"But we're never going to get to go, are we?"** It just hasn't happened yet, that's all, but it will. One way or the other, it's comin'. Don't ya feel it, Sally Mae? **"What? Feel what, Edie?"** A surprise...just wellin' up inside? Aunt June says if you believe like a mustard seed—that's enough. I figure that's about all the faith I got. See?

(She finds a freckle and points.)

The size of a freckle. **"Yer daddy ain't ever gonna let go of you. You know that."** Now you be quiet, Sally Mae. Just be quiet and believe. If that Mr. Arlie Ford should come over here tonight, and should he sneak like real

231

quick and try to give me a little kiss, do you suppose I should let him? Him just bein' so handsome and all? **"Edie, I don't think your daddy would go for that, not one little bit."** Shut up, Sally Mae, or I'm gonna have to stick a rag in your mouth.

ILLUSIONS
by Jonelle Grace

(EMILY, who has a history of drug and alcohol abuse, is temporarily staying at a youth shelter. As part of her treatment, she was asked by a counselor to draw two pictures—one reflecting the positive aspects of using drugs and the second reflecting the negative. In a private session, she responds to the counselor's question as to why she drew particular images. She picks up the first picture, studies it for a moment and then sets it back down.)

Emily

It's just a picture of me standing on a mountain—that's all. It doesn't mean anything. I mean, I don't know—I just... It's just how I felt—you know, when I was doing drugs. I felt like—like I was invincible—you know, like I had all this energy. I used to get high and run—I'd run all over town—at night mostly—I liked running at night. I felt like I could run forever, you know, just keep going and going—never stop.

(Pause. She picks up the second picture.)

This one's me just sitting there in my bedroom—you know, I'm just sitting on the floor. And this stuff here is— I don't know—I guess—see it didn't make sense. I couldn't figure out what was happening. I was doing a lot of speed and I had all this energy, but... It was like school, you know, I was studying all the time—I mean I

233

really studied. So, I couldn't figure it out—you know, why my grades kept dropping. Then this one night I'd been doing a lot of crank and I was really high, you know, and I thought—I mean my room was really messy and so I figured, why not clean it. I stayed up all night—I mean I wasn't sleepy 'cause I was really high and so I just kept on cleaning—all night long.

The next morning the alarm went off and...it was really weird because it was all still the same—my room I mean—it was just like it was when I started cleaning things up the night before. Like I said—I couldn't figure it out, you know, I mean I couldn't figure out why it was the same. And, then I saw it—this little pile in the corner—this pile of lint—you know, lint from the carpet—and then I looked at the floor and I knew why. It was clean—I mean, really clean—and that's when I knew... I knew that instead of cleaning my room, I just sat there on the floor all night long picking up pieces of lint. And, I thought—just for a minute I thought—I don't want to live like this.

MONEY & ME
by James Still

(A young woman of no specific age walks into the room and looks at the audience watching her. She looks at everyone, makes eye contact, and then begins talking.)

Young Woman

People used to walk by; people used to walk by or walk RIGHT through me. They didn't see my big hands, my little feet. My face that's not so beautiful. Do you like the shape of my lips? I have a hard time growing fingernails. I used to run the hurdles and everyone said I showed a lot of promise. I even won a gold medal once. I can make things. I know how to build a palace made of cardboard, I got a yard made of cracked cement and a flower garden made of memories. I got it all. A house, a yard, a dog. I didn't tell you about my dog? His name is Money.

(She gestures next to her.)

That's him.

(Looks at the audience.)

I know what you're thinking...sometimes I read people's minds for five dollars.

(She looks at Money.)

Money's head is green. He's read Charles Dickens. He has a bone-shaped tattoo. He sings old love songs. He has no desire to be famous or to have his own TV show. All those people looking at you.

(She looks around the audience.)

235

Looking right THROUGH you.

I never tell anybody my name, my weight, or my age. You tell 'em those things and before you know it you've told 'em your life story. It happens. Somebody wears that real interested look on his face and you feel so grateful your whole life just falls out of your mouth like a song in the shower. I might be seventeen, I might be seventy. I might weigh a pound, I might weigh a ton. Money and me met one night in the Metropolitan Museum of Art. It's in New York City. On Fifth Avenue. It's very fancy up on Fifth Avenue.

(Whispering.)

Rich people don't have interesting garbage. I like garbage that has EMOTION in it... I like to know it COST somebody something to throw it out.

A couple of years ago, during the winter when it was below zero for a month, I was so cold I thought my bones were going to break from walking so fast. There was a light on in the museum so I climbed the stairs nice and slow, and when no one was looking—I slipped inside. It was so warm. Then a guard started chasing me through all these rooms and just when it looked like he had me cornered, I just stopped—and pretended I was a sculpture. And it worked! The guard blew dust off my face. I didn't blink. People walked by and looked at me. I fell asleep standing up. When I woke up no one was looking at me. It was dark. Everyone had gone home. That's when I met Money the first time. I was listening to myself breathe and counting the dots on a painting by Roy Lichtenstein when out of nowhere I see this dog staring at a tortured painting by Pablo Picasso. In the darkness, this dog turned to me.

And winked. And then he looked back at the painting as if we'd known each other forever. Under his breath, he whispered, *"Creer usted en angeles?"* I stood with my mouth open and he must have known about my shaky Spanish because he turned back to me and repeated, "Do you believe in angels?" I nodded yes. I moved closer. Money curled up in my lap. And we became another painting in the Metropolitan Museum of Art.

(Looking at the audience.)
That's in New York City.

FAITH
by Jett Parsley

(MARY MASON, 18, is the daughter of a Pentecostal Holiness preacher who is very strict. She is telling this story to a young minister whom she has recently met and with whom she is falling in love.)

Mary Mason

When I was thirteen, we were goin' to this Pentecostal church. Not snake tamers, but... People were always seein' visions and speakin' in tongues, prophesizin'. One Wednesday-night meetin', Mama was sick and couldn't come with us, so Daddy took me and Daniel and John and Ruth alone. I was so worried about Mama I couldn't hardly concentrate on the service. The preacher was givin' a sermon about sickness and dyin', somethin' about how God could heal anyone who was saved but the sinners were bound for all kinds of skin-rottin' diseases. I just remember wantin' Mama to be there so bad, thinkin' what if God thought she was a sinner 'cause she wasn't at church, what if God made her even worse sick 'cause he was so mad at her. I don't know what all kinds of stuff I was thinkin' when somewhere in the church someone stood up and started blabberin'—speakin' in tongues. And then another and another and... the room was goin' wild, people interpretin' and shakin' and I was watchin' it all and thinkin', please God, please God, please God, and before I knew it I jumped up, too, and there were nonsense sounds fallin' out of my mouth, and my daddy was interpretin'—said I was sayin' hallelujah, glory to God, He's comin' back.

(Pause.)

I wasn't sayin' any of that. Daddy was so excited I'd been given the gift. I just felt like I was goin' to throw up. It wasn't tongues. I don't know what it was, but it wasn't tongues.

(Pause.)

I never told Daddy it wasn't.

ABOUT THE PLAYWRIGHTS

SANDRA FENICHEL ASHER's plays have been produced nationwide; 19 have been published including several favoring high school actors: **A Woman Called Truth; Dancing with Strangers; Across the Plains: The Journey of the Palace Wagon Family; Once, in the Time of Trolls;** and an adaptation of Jane Austen's **Emma** (all available from Dramatic Publishing). Also the author of 18 books for young readers, she is writer-in-residence at Drury College, serves as literary manager of Good Company Theater and teaches writing workshops throughout the country. In 1999 she received the American Alliance for Theatre and Education's Charlotte B. Chorpenning Playwright Award honoring a nationally known writer of outstanding plays for children. Asher is a member of The Dramatists Guild.

RIC AVERILL has been the artistic director and principal playwright for the Seem-To-Be Players in Lawrence, Kan., since he and his wife, Jeanne, founded the company 25 years ago. He was commissioned by the Kennedy Center to adapt **Alice in Wonderland** for a national tour in 1993-94, and in 1995 his original play, **Alex and the Shrink World**, was a winner of the Bonderman/IUPUI Youth Theatre Playwriting Symposium. In 1997, **Reliable Junk** was selected for development at the Bonderman Symposium, and won the American Alliance for Theatre and Education Unpublished Play Reading Competition and the Kansas Playwriting Fellowship. Averill is published by Dramatic Publishing and has contributed a chapter on playwriting for *Basic Drama Projects*, a Clark Publishing high school textbook by Fran Tanner.

MAX BUSH is a freelance playwright and director whose plays are widely produced on professional, educational and amateur stages across the country. His many honors include the Distinguished Play Award from the American Alliance for Theatre and Education, the Bonderman/IUPUI National Youth Theatre Playwriting Symposium, and Individual Artists grants from the Michigan Council for the Arts. In 1995 he received the American Alliance for Theatre and Education's Charlotte B. Chorpenning Playwright Award honoring a nationally known writer of outstanding plays for children. Ten of Bush's plays were anthologized in 1995 by Meriwether Press.

LINDA DAUGHERTY's plays have been produced by Stage One, the Louisville Children's Theatre, the Kennedy Center, Atlanta's Alliance Children's Theatre and the Dallas Children's Theatre. In 1999, she was honored with a Bonderman/IUPUI National Youth Theatre Playwriting Symposium Award to develop **Bless Cricket, Crest Toothpaste and Tommy Tune**. She has served as education director of the Dallas Children's Theater and has been developing arts curricula and teaching creative dramatics for over 30 years. As an actress, Daugherty has performed at the Seattle Repertory Theater, Indiana Repertory Theater and the Ivanhoe Theater in Chicago.

SILVIA GONZALEZ S. is a Mexican-American author who currently lives in Oregon with her husband. She is a weekly host for *Talk to Doc*, a medical information radio show, and works for *Plays on Tape and CD* published by Audio Theatre Publishing. A member of New Dramatists, she has won numerous awards: a 1990 INTAR Hispanic Playwright's Lab Award, a 1993 Kennedy Center New Visions/New Voices Award, and a 1994 South Coast Repertory's Hispanic Playwrights Project Award. She has twice received the Lee Korf Playwriting Award and an Honorable Mention in HBO's New Writer's Project.

JONELLE GRACE resides in Fayetteville, Ark., where she works as residency coordinator for the Walton Arts Center and director for Arts Live Theatre for Young Audiences. Since obtaining her M.F.A. in Playwriting from the University of Georgia, she has written 10 original plays, six of which have toured statewide with Arts Live Theatre's professional company. Grace also works extensively as an actress for both youth and adult theatre and is a member of ASSITEJ and The Dramatists Guild.

ALLISON GREGORY's first play, **Forcing Hyacinths,** won a Julie Harris Playwriting Award in 1994, and her children's play, **Even Steven Goes to War,** was selected by the Kennedy Center as part of its 1998 New Visions/ New Voices project. Several of her plays, including **Breathing Room, Scrambled Hot, Phantom Limb, Lucky** and **Interview,** have been staged by Theatre East and South Coast's Professional Conservatory. Gregory also works as a stage and television actor in Los Angeles and Seattle.

NANCY HANNA is a freelance advertising and radio writer who lives with her three children in the Chicago area. Her play, **Away the Bear,** won the 1997 Regent University One-Act Play Festival. Her 10-minute play, **Rush to Judgment,** was produced at the Dallas Theatre Center where she was a member of the Dallas Playwright Project. She has taught acting at the Plano Children's Theatre where she has also written and directed her plays.

ELEANOR HARDER is the author, composer/lyricist of 16 published plays and musicals. She is a member of The Dramatists Guild, Actors' Equity, AFTRA, ASCAP and PEN. She has been honored by the Los Angeles Board of Education for creating music and literature for family audiences, is the recipient of a Michigan state grant for original music, and was selected for the Best Teacher of the Year Award from UCLA's Writers' Program. She has also written children's novels, stories for Hanna-Barbera TV Productions, film strips for CBS and stories and songs for Mattel Toys.

JOANNA H. KRAUS is an award-winning playwright of 14 published and widely produced scripts throughout the United States, Canada, England and Australia. **The Ice Wolf** and **Remember My Name** were produced off-off-Broadway before being anthologized and published by New Plays and Samuel French. She has won first place in the Bonderman/IUPUI National Youth Theatre Playwriting Symposium, and was commissioned by the Honor of Humanity Project to write **Angel in the Night** under the direction of National-Louis University in affiliation with the Avenue of the Righteous. It won the 1996 Distinguished Play Award from the American Alliance for Theatre and Education and is published by Dramatic Publishing.

JOHN O'BRIEN is a graduate of Tufts University, magna cum laude, Phi Beta Kappa. After 35 years of teaching English and theatre at the public school level, he now teaches playwriting at an adult education center in the Boston area. A finalist at the O'Neill Theater Festival, O'Brien is the author of 13 published plays, nine of which are published by Dramatic Publishing.

JETT PARSLEY received her A.B in English from Duke University and her M.F.A. in Dramatic Writing from New York University's Tisch School of the Arts. Her plays include **Right Side Wrong, First Born, Stuck, More Than Meets the Eye, Up a Sycamore Tree** and **Volatile Combinations. Locked Doors and Lightning Bugs** received the Southeastern Theatre Conference's Charles M. Getchell Award and was a winner of the Charlotte Repertory Theatre's New Plays in America Festival.

It was included in the 1993 Eugene O'Neill National Playwrights' Conference. She has attended the Mt. Sequoyah New Play Retreat and has had her works produced by the Raleigh Ensemble Theatre and the Playwrights Theatre of New Jersey. She is the recipient of an Emerging Artists's Grant from the Durham Arts Council and teaches high school English and creative writing in Durham, N. C.

MARK PLAISS lives in La Porte, Ind., with his wife and two children. His short play, **Horseshoe Bend**, was included in **Short Stuff: Ten- to Twenty-Minute Plays for Mature Actors** published by Dramatic Publishing. He has written for the *New York Daily News*, the *Chicago Tribune* and the *Sacramento Bee*.

STEVEN SATER has written for theater, television and film. His off-Broadway and regional stage credits include **Carbondale Dreams** (Dramatists Play Service); **Perfect for You, Doll** (Rosenthal Prize Winner—Cincinnati Playhouse); **Asylum** (Greenwich Street Theatre); **Pearl's Tears** (George R. Kernodle Prize Winner; J.C.C. of Houston); **Umbrage** (Steppenwolf New Play Prize); **In Search of Lost Wings** (Sanford Meisner Center); and **The Plains of Ilion** (Miniature Theatre of Chester; University of Arkansas).

MICHAEL SCHNEIDER is a graduate of Northwestern University's School of Speech. He is the author of **Learn Me Somethin'**, published in the September 1996 issue of *Dramatics* magazine and by Dramatic Publishing. From 1980-1996, Schneider taught acting, playwriting, dramatic literature and math at Rochester, N. Y.'s, School of the Arts. The works featured in this anthology were written as exercises and short performance pieces for his students. Schneider currently lives near Sisters, Ore., where he writes and teaches skiing.

LAURA SHAMAS has written 20 plays including **Portrait of a Nude, Saucer City, Amelia Lives, The Other Shakespeare** and **Picnic at Hanging Rock** (adaptation). She has won awards for playwriting including a Drama-Logue Award, a Fringe First Award, the Warner Brothers Award, and a Mary Roberts Rinehart Foundation Award. She teaches at Pepperdine University and lives in the Los Angeles area.

TED SOD's plays include **Stealing, Damaged Goods, A Rude Awakening, Dialogues of the Seattleites** and **Make Me Pelé for a Day.** His honors include a Eugene O'Neill Theatre Center's Opera/Music Theatre Conference Award, a Washington state Arts Commission Playwriting Fellowship and grants from PEN Center USA and The Edward Albee Foundation. He has served as artist-in-residence at Seattle Repertory and currently is Artistic Associate/Director of Education and Outreach at George Street Playhouse.

JAMES STILL's award-winning plays have been produced at theaters throughout the United States, Canada and Puerto Rico. His plays include **Hush: An Interview with America, Just Before Sleep, Jack Frost, And Then They Came for Me, The Velocity of Gary, The Velveteen Rabbit, Amber Waves** and **The Secret History of the Future.** He is the recipient of a TCG/Pew Charitable Trust National Theatre Artist Grant with Indiana Repertory Theatre and the American Alliance for Theatre and Education's Charlotte B. Chorpenning Playwright Award honoring a nationally known writer of outstanding plays for children.

CARIDAD SVICH is a playwright/poet and translator of Cuban, Argentine, Croation and Spanish descent. Her works include **But There Are Fires, Gleaning/Rebusca, Scar, Any Place But Here, Pensacola** and **Alchemy of**

Desire/Dead-Man's Blues. Her work has been produced at London's Royal Court Theatre, The Women's Project in New York City, the Mark Taper Forum, the Lincoln Center and at New York's Theater for a New City. She has been a visiting lecturer at the Yale School of Drama and has served as playwright-in-residence at INTAR, South Coast Repertory's Hispanic Playwrights Project and the A.S.K. Theater Projects in Los Angeles. Her critical writing has been featured in *American Theatre, Dramatists Quarterly*, and *Contemporary Theatre Review/UK*. She is currently a resident playwright at the Mark Taper Forum Theatre in Los Angeles.

MIKE THOMAS is a playwright, actor and director who resides in Fayetteville, Ark. After receiving a degree in Drama from the University of Arkansas, Fayetteville, Thomas spent several years in Los Angeles acting in commercials and directing plays. He is currently an elementary school teacher and continues to act and direct. He played a feature role in the film *The White River Kid*, with Antonio Banderas and Bob Hoskins. His writing is included in **A Grand Entrance: Scenes and Monologues for Mature Actors** published by Dramatic Publishing.

ELIZABETH WONG's plays, including **Letters to a Student Revolutionary** and **Kimchee and Chitlins**, have been produced professionally off-Broadway, in Atlanta, Los Angles, Chicago, Philadelphia, Singapore and Tokyo. She has received commissions from the Kennedy Center for the Performing Arts, the Denver Center Theatre, Omaha Magic Theatre and Actors Theatre of Louisville. She has written for television, has been an op/ed columnist for the *Los Angeles Times* and has taught playwriting at USC and UC Santa Barbara. In 1999, she served as a member of the Kennedy Center/American College Theatre Festival National Selection Team.

PERMISSION ACKNOWLEDGMENTS

inquiries should be addressed to Mark Plaiss, 4137 W. Andrea, La Porte IN 46350.

WAY OF THE WORLD by Max Bush. Copyright 1999 by Max Bush. Reprinted by permission of the author. Excerpted from SARAH by Max Bush, copyright 1997. All inquiries should be addressed to Max Bush, 5372 132nd Ave., Hamilton MI 49419

WE ALWAYS FIND YOU by Silvia Gonzalez S. Copyright 1999 by Silvia Gonzalez S. Reprinted by permission of the author. Excerpted from BOXCAR by Silvia Gonzalez S., copyright 1989. All inquiries should be addressed to Cheri Magid, Literary Dept., New Dramatists, 424 W. 44th St., New York NY 10036.

WELCOME TO MCDONALD'S by Michael Schneider. Copyright 1999 by Michael Schneider. Reprinted by permission of the author. All inquiries should be addressed to Michael Schneider, 17614 Plainview Rd., Bend OR 97701.

WHAT'S WRONG WITH HIM? by Linda Daugherty. Copyright 1999 by Linda Daugherty. Reprinted by permission of the author. Excerpted from BLESS CRICKET, CREST TOOTHPASTE AND TOMMY TUNE by Linda Daugherty, copyright 1998. All inquiries should be addressed to Linda or Paul Daugherty, 7027 Fisher Rd., Dallas TX 75214.

WHO WANTSTA KNOW? by John O'Brien. Copyright 1999 by John O'Brien. Reprinted by permission of the author. All inquiries should be addressed to John O'Brien, 41 Delle Ave., Boston MA 02120.

X-MAN by Silvia Gonzalez S. Copyright 1999 by Silvia Gonzalez S. Reprinted by permission of the author. All inquiries should be addressed to Cheri Magid, Literary Dept., New Dramatists, 424 W. 44th St., New York NY 10036.